CW00524882

1991

91

'4

Mr Browser
in the
Space Museum

Andersen Young Readers' Library

Mr Browser
in the
Space Museum

Philip Curtis
Illustrated by Tony Ross

WITHDRAWN FOR SALE

NANTWICH

K 0520

Andersen Press · London

First published in 1985 by
Andersen Press Limited,
19-21 Conway Street,
London W1

All rights reserved. No part of this publication may be reproduced,
stored in a retrieval system, or transmitted in any form or by any
means, electronic, mechanical, photocopying, recording or otherwise,
without the written permission of the publisher.

© Text 1985 by Philip Curtis
© Illustrations 1985 by Andersen Press Limited

British Library Cataloguing in Publication Data

Curtis Philip
  Mr Browser in the space museum.—(Andersen young readers'
  library)
  I. Title
  823'.914[J]   PZ7

ISBN 0 86264 095 4

WITHDRAWN FOR SALE

Printed and bound in Great Britain by Anchor Brendon Ltd.,
Tiptree, Essex.

Contents

1	Chivvy Chase After Dark	7
2	Mr Watchett is Scared	21
3	Mr Browser's River Trip	34
4	The Kingdom of the Kiswastis	51
5	Mr Watchett Speaks Up	68
6	The Museum of Other Worlds	80
7	Spots of Trouble for Spiky	99
8	An Art Lesson in Space	114
9	Reunion in Space	125

1

Chivvy Chase After Dark

'I could have gone on swimming all night,' said
Spiky Jackson as he was on his way home from the
local swimming pool with his friend Michael
Fairlie. 'I reckon I could swim the English Channel on a calm day.'

'On a calm day with an engine attached to you,'
Michael joked.

It was already dark by the time they saw Chivvy
Chase School ahead of them, looming like a black
monster on the corner of two roads. Mrs Fairlie
only allowed Michael to visit the pool in the
evening on condition that he returned with Spiky.

'What time is it, Mike?' asked Spiky, and Michael looked closely at his watch.

'Twenty-five past six.'

'If we don't hurry, I shall miss my favourite T.V.
programme.' Spiky was tired after his long distance efforts in the pool.

They quickened their pace, but still he wasn't
satisfied.

'It's a bore, having to go right round the school,'
he said. 'There's a hole in the railings—why not
take a short cut across the field and the playground and out on the other side? That'll save
about five minutes.'

7

'You know how mad old Sage was with those Comprehensive School kids who used the field as a short cut,' said Michael, shaking his head. 'He threatened to call in the police if anyone else was found trespassing.'

'We wouldn't be trespassing,' argued Spiky. 'It's our school, isn't it?'

By the time Michael had worked out an answer to this reasoning, the hole on the fence loomed up large alongside them.

'Come on,' urged Spiky. 'No one will see us. There's only a hedge to crawl through on the other side. We can keep close to the building.'

He stopped for a second to wait for the hesitant Michael, then decided that deeds were more persuasive than words, and pulled himself through the hole. As he had hoped, Michael decided against being left alone, and hastily followed him. They ran hard across the field, and only paused for breath when they could lean against the wall of the main school building.

'There you are,' panted Spiky. 'It's easy. I'm going between the school and the demountable classrooms—no one will see us there.'

Three extra classrooms had been placed alongside the school some years back when the number of children at Chivvy Chase had increased. Spiky moved along beside their dark, wooden walls.

'It's fun to be in school when you ought not to

be!' he whispered.

'Quiet!' Michael whispered back. 'I thought I heard something.'

'You're imagining it,' scoffed Spiky. 'There can't be anybody else here.'

Then he, too, heard the noise—a sound as if something were being dragged across the ground.

'It's coming from near the caretaker's shed,' said Michael.

'Something banging in the wind?' suggested Spiky without much hope. Michael shook his head.

'There's hardly any wind,' he said. They edged

their way to the end of the last outside classroom, knowing that from there they would have a view of the shed which Mr Watchett, the caretaker, used to store unwanted furniture and other items.

The main building of the school took a left turn at this point, so that with the end wall of the last outside classroom and the shed it formed three sides of a grassy square. Michael and Spiky peered round the corner of the classroom. Their mouths opened, but they did not speak.

Mr Watchett, the caretaker, was busily dragging an old desk out of the shed. They watched as he pulled it to the centre of the grassy square, where he left it alongside four more which he had already dragged there. He went back into the shed and could be heard pushing and pulling at yet another one. The boys stared at each other in disbelief.

'What's he doing that for?' asked Michael.

'Don't know—but I've never seen him work so hard,' whispered Spiky.

Mr Watchett was certainly devoted to his task. He edged the next desk out of the doorway, and soon had it standing alongside the others. The boys stayed until ten desks were standing together in the open, and Mr Watchett was considering whether to put the next one on top of the others. By now he was puffing and panting, but he showed no signs of giving up.

'You're missing your programme,' whispered Michael.

'Doesn't matter,' said Spiky, showing that the real world can be much more interesting than television. 'But we'd better be going, or my mum will be mad.'

'We'd better go back and round the other side of the classrooms,' suggested Michael. Spiky nodded—but as he turned he kicked against one of the brick blocks supporting the classrooms.

'Ouch!' he cried.

In a flash Michael saw Mr Watchett look up, then he ducked alongside Spiky and started to creep away along the classroom wall. After a while they stopped and listened. Clearly came the sound of another desk scraping along the ground.

'It's okay,' said Spiky, relieved.

'But he heard you,' insisted Michael. 'I saw his face. Yet he hasn't come after us—it's not like old Watchett!'

'It's not like old Watchett to be working hard at nearly seven o'clock at night, dragging old desks about,' observed Spiky. 'But I'm not going to introduce ourselves to him. Let's be going!'

Their exit from the school grounds was now a simple one. They felt safer in the knowledge that the caretaker was fully occupied in his new pursuit of dragging desks about in the darkness. Their short cut had cost them a quarter of an hour at least of lost time, and they couldn't explain to their parents why they were later home than usual. The Jackson and Fairlie parents grumbled a little about the swimming instructor keeping their children so late, and the boys rather guiltily allowed him to take the blame.

On their way to school the next day Spiky returned to the subject of the desks.

'Wonder if they'll still be there this morning?' he pondered.

'Of course they will be,' said Michael. 'You don't imagine old Watchett would drag them all back again on the same evening, do you? He's probably had to put them out so that a carpenter can take them away for repairing.'

'Watchett usually does them himself,' said Spiky, but since Michael was not an interested listener he forgot about the desks and gave his mind up to wondering whether he should exchange his best marble for Martin Portland-Smythe's old tennis ball.

'At least we'll be able to play football at break if you do,' Michael urged him.

'But it's not really worth it,' mused Spiky. 'His tennis ball is ordinary, my marble is special.'

When they entered the playground he remembered the desks again.

'I'm going to have a look at them,' he said.

'It's out of bounds,' Michael warned him, but

Spiky was off between the outside classrooms and the school hall. A minute later he came speeding back as if shot from a bow.

'They're gone!' he shouted to Michael. 'There isn't one of them left!'

Michael was more interested in claiming a place on the crowded climbing frame, and quickly found a reason for the departure of the desks.

'I suppose they've come with a lorry and taken them away already,' he remarked.

'What? A lorry come to school before nine o'clock in the morning? That's not likely,' objected Spiky.

'Then what is likely?' countered Michael, and Spiky couldn't answer that, so they spent the rest of the time before the bell rang hanging upside down on the climbing frame, which perhaps helped to clear their brains for the morning's work.

As they walked into school, Spiky overheard a snatch of conversation between Anna Cardwell and her friend Jennifer, without paying a great deal of attention to them.

'Did you hear that bang in the middle of the night?' asked Anna, and Jennifer shook her head. 'It was loud enough to wake me up,' went on Anna. 'I got out of bed and went to the window, but I couldn't see anything.'

'Maybe it was thunder,' suggested Jennifer.

'I don't think so. I didn't see any lightning, and there wasn't a sound after that.'

'Perhaps a plane passing through the sound barrier,' guessed Jennifer.

'It was very sharp, like the firing of a big gun,' said Anna thoughtfully.

'It didn't disturb me,' declared Jennifer, to close the subject.

'I heard it too,' put in Andrea Long unexpectedly, 'but I just turned over and went to sleep again. It came from somewhere near the school.'

'I couldn't fall asleep for a long time after that,' said Anna with a yawn. 'I'm sure I'll fall asleep in school today.'

Spiky was just considering that Anna and Andrea both lived very near the school, whereas Jennifer's home was over a mile away, when he arrived in class to find Mr Browser waiting to make a prompt start to the school day. Spiky was kept too busy to think about vanished desks or strange noises in the night, but maybe deep in his mind he was still conscious of the vanished pile of desks—or perhaps he just chanced to work away at the unscrewing of the seat of his own desk as Mr Browser carried on about the Spanish Armada. Whatever the reason for his secret activity, it resulted in the seat clattering on the floor, with Spiky on top of it, just as the Spanish Armada was entering the English Channel.

Mr Browser was not pleased.

'Sit next to Michael for the rest of the lesson,' he told Spiky, 'and please don't interrupt English history again. At playtime, go next door and borrow Mr Caracco's screwdriver, and I'll fix the seat on again.'

Unfortunately, when break came, Mr Browser discovered that the task was not so easy. Two of the four screws were missing, and a third one was twisted out of shape. Annoyed, Mr Browser was determined to find a solution, because he far preferred to have Spiky sitting on his own.

'I'll find Mr Sage and ask him if there is a spare desk for you,' he said. 'Bring Michael so that you two can carry the new one up and then take the old one to Mr Watchett's shed for repair.'

They followed him to Mr Sage's room, where the Headmaster had just finished his coffee and was in pleasant enough mood.

'So, Simon Jackson, you've been breaking up the furniture, have you?'

'No sir, please, I only unscrewed the last screw while I was listening to Mr Browser, I did it without thinking, and the desk has had screws missing for a long time—'

'Oh yes, Simon. Excuses, excuses,' said Mr Sage cheerfully. 'Well, as a punishment you'll have to sit at one of those old desks which have been taken out of use, if we can find one firm enough. There aren't any more desks in the school—we're going over to tables and chairs, you know.'

Mr Browser frowned. He liked the old-fashioned desks much better, because he knew how untidy children's belongings can become on tables. He kept silent and followed Mr Sage to the caretaker's shed.

Mr Sage took out his bunch of keys and found the one which fitted.

'Great Scott!' he said as he opened the door.

17

'No desks,' said Mr Browser. 'Only old chairs at the back.'

'There should be thirty old desks in the front here,' said Mr Sage, flinging the door wide open. 'County said they would come and take them away. I must see Mr Watchett about it. I'm always told before things are taken. Boys, find Mr Watchett for me, please.'

Mr Watchett was easily found. He was sitting behind a big mug of tea in his boiler room.

'Mr Sage wants you, Mr Watchett,' said Spiky. 'It's about the desks,' he added.

'Desks?' said Mr Watchett. 'Don't know what he's on about. Oh, well, I may as well come and see him.'

'The desks,' called out Mr Sage as soon as he saw the caretaker. 'They've all gone. What have you done with them?'

'Me?' said Mr Watchett, confused. 'I ain't done nothing. Why, they must have come and took them away without letting me know!'

'They don't do that,' said Mr Sage sternly. 'They have to let me know first.'

'Well, I've done nothing with them,' persisted the caretaker obstinately.

'But I saw them yesterday night, out on the grass here—' burst out Spiky, and stopped short suddenly as he realised that he would have to explain about the short cut to Mr Sage.

18

'You must 'ave been dreaming, boy,' said the caretaker, giving Spiky a nasty look.

'What do you mean, Simon?' asked Mr Browser, and Mr Sage rattled his keys impatiently.

'Well—er—maybe I made a mistake,' said Spiky. 'It was shortly after school—I mean it would have been a mistake.'

He ended in miserable, red-faced confusion, and Mr Watchett took quick advantage.

'Were you wanting a desk, Mr Sage?' he asked.

'This boy has broken the seat of his,' said Mr Sage, pointing at Spiky irritably.

'Leave it to me, Mr Sage,' promised the caretaker. 'I'll have it done by twelve o'clock.'

'Thanks very much, Mr Watchett,' said Mr Browser. 'You boys can go to the playground now.'

Michael and Spiky ran off, pleased to have escaped Mr Sage's anger.

'You nearly gave us away, Spiky,' said Michael.

'I know,' admitted Spiky. 'But Watchett has lied about the desks, hasn't he! We didn't dream it, Mike, did we?'

'No,' Michael reassured him. 'Mr Watchett has acted very strangely last night and this morning. Spiky, suppose he was hypnotised last night? Then he wouldn't remember what happened, would he?'

'I suppose not,' agreed Spiky. 'But who would want to hypnotise him for a few old desks?'

Michael was beaten.

'No one I can think of,' he admitted. 'Let's see if we can join in a game of football.'

They ran to the playground, only to be greeted by the sound of the bell for the end of break.

2

Mr Watchett is Scared

Mr Sage was so busy with a hundred and one different problems that he preferred to forget about the old desks, which were of no more use to him or the school. He was busy signing an order for more coloured paper and powder paint when his secretary, Miss Copewell, interrupted him.

'Well?' asked Mr Sage, trying to keep his finger on the right place on the complicated long form.

'I'm sorry to bother you,' said Miss Copewell, but I feel I must tell you that people are becoming very careless round here.'

'People? What people?'

'Well—er—the teachers,' said Miss Copewell.

'Is that new?' asked Mr Sage a little unfairly.

'No—well, it really is too bad, Mr Sage. Over a hundred writing books have disappeared from the stock room, and Miss Causewell is complaining that she can't find the drawing boards. Mr Caracco has lost the cassette recorder in his room, and Mr Browser's blackboard ruler has disappeared. A number of other small items are missing as well. You really should come and look at the stock room, Mr Sage. It's half empty!'

'Oh no! They must have been allowing children in there again!' grumbled Mr Sage, and followed

her into the hall and opened the stock room door. Miss Copewell waited while his sharp eyes told him the truth.

'There's only half the paper there used to be!' he said. 'And look at this box of felt pens—it's nearly empty. This is—is unforgivable!'

He was still staring at the depleted shelves when Spiky Jackson knocked on the door.

'Yes, dear?' Miss Copewell greeted him.

'Please, Miss, Mr Browser says could he have a spare blackboard compass, because the one in his cupboard is missing.'

'Missing?' cried Mr Sage from inside the store

room. 'What has he done with it? Things like that can't go missing!'

Spiky coughed.

'We've lost a lot of scissors lately, and Mr Browser's blackboard ruler—and some books from the shelves,' he said. 'Mr Browser can't understand it at all.'

'Nor can I,' said Mr Sage severely. 'Miss Copewell, I shall have to call an emergency staff meeting this afternoon. This sort of thing just can't go on! We have to fight for every little bit we are given, because money is so short, and it's all being lost through carelessness.'

'Yes, Mr Sage,' said Miss Copewell. 'What time do you want the meeting?'

Spiky coughed again.

'Oh, find him a blackboard compass,' ordered Mr Sage grumpily, and stalked back to his room. Spiky hurried back to class with the blackboard compass, which Mr Browser received gratefully.

'There are lots of things missing in the stock cupboard too, Mr Browser,' said Spiky cheerfully, but Mr Browser ignored him and drew a large circle on the blackboard.

Spiky sat there pretending to listen to Mr Browser's explanation of the difference between a radius and a diameter, but he was concentrating more on an idea which was taking possession of his mind. He couldn't share the idea with anybody until the end of the morning, when he grabbed Michael Fairlie by the arm and rushed him off to a quiet corner of the playground.

'There's stacks of stuff missing in the stock room,' he told Michael. 'Other teachers have lost things, and think of all the books that have gone from our room.'

'So what?' said Michael bluntly; he didn't care much what happened to the school's belongings, and he couldn't understand why Spiky was becoming so excited.

'I think old Watchett is robbing the school,' declared Spiky. 'All these missing objects are going the same way as the old desks, I bet you.'

'You can't prove it,' objected Michael. 'Old Watchett is always complaining, but I don't think he's dishonest. He always gives us our footballs back when they go on the roof.'

Spiky was not to be put off.

'There's going to be a staff meeting after school about the missing things, and Watchett will be across at the Infants' School clearing up then. I'm going to take a look inside his shed at that time. I've a feeling some of those missing things might be tucked away there, waiting for him to sell them off. Will you come with me?'

'Okay,' agreed Michael without much enthusiasm. 'It'll be a waste of time, I'm sure.'

So Spiky and Michael played around in the

playground after school, and no teachers came to send them off home, because the teachers were all listening to a lecture by Mr Sage on how everyone must pull together and see that materials were not wasted nor lost.

'Now!' said Spiky suddenly, and they crept along the same route they had taken on the night when they'd seen all the desks on the grass. They edged round the corner and stood still in surprise. The door of the shed was open, and Mr Watchett was frantically pulling all the old chairs to the front of it. Fascinated, Spiky moved forward to try to make out what some boxes behind the chairs contained. As if he had a sixth sense, Mr Watchett turned and stared at the boys. A look of irritation and confusion crossed his face, then he snapped into speech.

'What are you doing here, you boys? Hop it at once, or I'll report you to Mr Sage!'

He took a pace forward as though he meant to come and grab hold of them. He looked so fierce that they instantly turned and ran, and only slowed into a walk when they were outside the school gate.

'There you are!' declared Spiky. 'I told you something fishy is going on. He knew about the staff meeting, and thought it would be a safe time to start moving the chairs.'

'But why?' asked Michael.

25

'That we have to find out. I wouldn't be surprised if he won't bring those chairs out tonight
with some of the other things and get rid of them.
Yes, I reckon something's going to happen tonight, Mike. Will you call for me and we'll try and
find out? Seven o'clock at my place. Oh, come on,
your parents won't miss you for an hour or so. Tell
them we're going to play some video games,

26

or something.'

Michael was easily won over, and at seven o'clock Spiky met him at the end of his road and they trotted all the way to the hole in the school railings. The night was dark and cloudy, and they slipped calmly into the school field and across it to the playground.

'Can't hear anything,' whispered Michael. 'What shall we do if nothing has happened?'

'I shall shine my torch through a gap in the back of the shed, to see what's in those boxes,' said Spiky.

But when they rounded the corner of the outside classroom they saw that something had already happened. Out on the grass the old chairs were piled, and next to them the boxes. The shed door was closed, and Mr Watchett was nowhere to be seen.

'Told you,' said Spiky. 'Now I'm going to find out what's in the boxes.'

He moved silently across the grass, followed by Michael, and shone his torch into one of the boxes.

'Look! Boxes of chalk, felt pens, packets of coloured paper—and there's Mr Caracco's missing cassette recorder. Now we know, Mike! Old Watchett's no better than a robber!'

'What shall we do, Spiky?' asked Michael, but there was no time for an answer. Michael's collar was gripped by a firm hand, and he saw Spiky jerk back suddenly.

'You young idiots!' came the voice of Mr Watchett. 'Don't you know you're in deadly danger? Into the shed, quick, or it could be the end for all of us! It's coming any minute now!'

He pushed and pulled them frantically toward the shed door, shoved them against it and they all fell inside. Immediately he closed the door, and they could see he was trembling as he stood there white-faced before them. They scrambled to their feet.

'What's coming, Mr Watchett?' asked Spiky.

'If you'd stayed there, my lad, you might have been scooped up with all that junk out there,' replied Mr Watchett. 'You'd never 'ave been 'eard of again, you wouldn't. What on earth brings you poking about around here, where you ought not to be?'

'It's all school property, Mr Watchett,' pointed out Spiky, speaking a little bit in the style of Mr Sage. Mr Watchett managed a feeble smile.

'So it was, my boy. Used to be, but it ain't any more. No way. You'd best start praying that they don't get mad with you and take us and the shed and all.'

'They? Who?' asked Michael, but Watchett was listening for something else.

'First there comes a sort of bang,' he said,

talking chiefly to himself, 'and then a kind of wind, and then this great claw comes down. Oh, why did I ever come to work in this forsaken place?'

Mr Watchett was looking so old and trembly that both boys found to their surprise that they were beginning to feel sorry for him. Perhaps the effort of carrying so many desks and chairs over the years had affected his brain.

'How do you know these people are coming now?' Spiky asked him.

'They tell me,' answered the caretaker, looking dazed. 'They come at night, mostly, and wake me up, and tell me what to do.'

'But what do they want with old desks and chairs?' asked Michael.

'Come to the back of the shed,' said Mr Watchett. 'We don't want to be carried off in that great claw, do we! Any moment now—'

As they obeyed him and made for the far end of the shed, a sharp bang from high above them made them jump.

'Down!' cried Mr Watchett in terror, and threw himself flat on the floor. Spikey had time to remember that Anna had reported hearing a similar sound. He followed Mr Watchett's example, and put his hands over his ears to stifle another growing sound—that of an ever increasing wind, descending upon them like a tornado. The walls and door of the shed creaked,

29

and soon, unable to resist any longer the rusted hinges of the door gave way and the door blew into the shed.

Scared, Michael and Spiky looked up to see if they needed to protect themselves, but quickly forgot their own possible danger when they saw what was happening outside. A huge claw-like object, a colossal grab, was descending with open jaws upon the chairs and the boxes. Like a hungry shark it snapped its jaws to, and in one mouthful had swallowed the chairs and the boxes and begun to ascend.

The sound of the wind came again, but this time the current must have been directed upwards, for apart from a sucking of air out through the empty doorway the boys felt no ill effects. Mr Watchett opened his eyes and looked around him warily.

'It's gone,' said Spiky, 'and so have the chairs and the boxes.'

'Thank heavens!' said Mr Watchett, and scrambled to his feet. They went out to the spot where the chairs had been, and Spiky shone his torch on the grass.

'One or two marks,' he said, 'but there's nothing much to show what happened.'

'They'd never believe me if I told,' muttered Mr Watchett. 'They'd think I'd gone mad, or more likely that I was trying to rob the school.

But what would I want with old desks and chairs?'

'We saw it,' said Michael, thinking to comfort him. 'We'll back you up, won't we, Spiky?'

'Surely,' agreed Spiky, but Mr Watchett was not at all pleased. As if he had suddenly realised the danger brought close to him by the boys' knowledge, he turned on them fiercely.

'I know you've seen it,' he said, 'and you must promise me that you won't say anything about it! You dare not say anything, because if you do, that thing may come back and carry us all away. They made me promise not to say anything. Will you do the same? Please, lads!' begged Mr Watchett.

It was a strange and moving sight to see this hard-working man, usually so strict, pleading with a couple of boys for help. They were so scared themselves that they needed little persuading.

'We promise we won't tell,' said Spiky, and Mike nodded agreement.

'Good lads,' said Mr Watchett, sighing with relief. 'Come to me tomorrow morning and I'll give you all the unclaimed old tennis balls in my boiler room.'

It was the best he could do for them, and they hurried home at his request without delay. But the further they were away from the school, the harder they knew it would be to keep this strange secret.

'What on earth do you suppose it was?' asked Spiky, pausing for breath. Michael looked at Spiky and then up to the sky, and didn't know what to reply.

'One thing's sure,' said Spiky, 'I'm not risking a short cut through the school field at night any more. I wouldn't like to be caught in that horrible claw-like grab!'

'Nor I,' agreed Michael, and they spoke no more as they hurried home, thinking all the way.

3

Mr Browser's River Trip

Spiky Jackson was not one to allow the chance of a free gift to pass him by, and at break the next day he persuaded Michael to leave the playground and confront Mr Watchett in his boiler room. Mr Watchett, who also happened to be having his break, was sitting behind a newspaper with a mug of tea on the table. He greeted the boys in his usual suspicious manner.

'Well you boys—what may you be after?'

'We've come for the old tennis balls you promised us, Mr Watchett,' said Spiky.

'Old tennis balls?' For a moment they thought the caretaker was going to deny all knowledge of his promise, but he suddenly folded his newspaper and smiled at them.

'Ah! Last night!' he said. 'Good lads. Not said a word, have you?'

'No, Mr Watchett.'

'All right, then.'

He rummaged in a cardboard box on the floor under the table, and brought out four ancient, balding tennis balls.

"Ere you are, then. Two each. And maybe in a couple of weeks' time I'll have one or two more, if you keeps your part of the bargain.'

'Yes, Mr Watchett. Thanks a lot. We'll keep our mouths shut!'

'I wouldn't show them tennis balls to the other kids all at once,' advised Mr Watchett. 'Put 'em in your pockets. And now be off with you.'

He returned to his newspaper and his tea.

'We're on to a good thing!' said Spiky as they ran back to the playground.'

'Yes,' agreed Michael. 'But I still wonder if we shouldn't tell Mr Sage.'

'Why? It's not as though Mr Watchett has stolen anything. And who would believe us if we told? Let them find out for themselves, I say.'

Michael was easily convinced, and they started some shooting practice against the railings with one of the newly gained tennis balls.

While these secret activities were going on unknown to Mr Sage, the Headmaster was vainly searching for his cane, which usually stood unused in a corner of his room, hidden by a cupboard. Mr Sage seldom used the cane, but he found it useful to keep it there, and on one or two occasions he brought it out and whacked it on his table to encourage boys to own up to their misdeeds. He had a suitable case for this treatment in mind, and was highly puzzled when he discovered that the cane was not in its proper place. It was extra annoying to him that it had disappeared so soon after his meeting to tell the teachers to be careful with school materials, for now he couldn't very well ask around for it. In any case it was most unlikely that anyone else would have taken it; no one but Mr Sage was allowed to use it, and none of the teachers would want to do so. There was only one person in whom he could confide, and she came into the room at that very moment with the second post.

'Miss Copewell,' he said irritably, 'you haven't seen my cane, have you? It's missing.'

'Of course I haven't seen it, Mr Sage.' Miss Copewell laughed and handed over the post. 'Not very interesting post, I think—except perhaps this one from the River Boat Company.'

'I'll look at it now,' said Mr Sage, and when he had read the letter he rubbed his hands together with satisfaction.

'Just the thing for Mr Browser, don't you think?' he said and tossed the letter to Miss Copewell.

'Dear Sir,' she read. 'It is with pleasure that I am able to inform you that we have acquired a vessel which will be able to ply on the River Graywater next summer, and we are making one or two testing voyages before winter sets in, so that we can assess the exact length of the trip and find out how to help schools to gain most from the experience. The boat will pass through a lock and will sail as far as the estuary of the river before turning back. For these introductory sailings we are prepared to charge only fifty pence per child. Please let us know as soon as possible if you wish to take up this offer. The trip will last about two and a half hours, and drinks will be available on board.'

'Sounds good,' agreed Miss Copewell. 'Mr Browser's been talking about locks. I saw a drawing of one on his blackboard.'

'Exactly,' said Mr Sage. 'It won't hurt the children to see a real one, will it! I'll take the letter up to him myself, immediately after play. By the way, someone will have to go with him—how would you like an afternoon on the river yourself?'

'I'll think about it,' said Miss Copewell. As soon as the children had returned to their classes, Mr Sage took the letter up to Mr Browser, and forgot all about his missing cane.

Mr Browser received the invitation without a great deal of enthusiasm.

'It's late in the year,' he said. 'It might rain.'

'Oh, it says here that there is covered accommodation,' Mr Sage assured him. 'Have you any other visits planned for your class?'

Mr Browser hadn't, so that settled it. A week later Class 8, accompanied by Mr Browser and Miss Copewell, climbed into a coach which was to take them to the River Graywater, a small river which trickled between fields and marshes out to join the North Sea.

'Cor!' exclaimed Spiky Jackson when the River

Boat Company's vessel came into sight. 'That boat's on its last legs!'

'Boats don't have legs!' said Miss Copewell critically, but she had to agree that the vessel didn't look, to put it in sailor's terms, all that shipshape. It was rusty, and the awning which was to provide cover in case of rain had a large tear in it. Only the name looked freshly painted.

'*Kiswasti*,' read Anna Cardwell. 'That's a funny name!'

'Very odd,' said Miss Copewell as they lined up on the small landing stage.

'Please Miss! Please Miss!' The voice was that of Ali Khan, the newest and quietest member of the class, whose parents had come to England from Pakistan years ago, and had just taken over a newsagent's shop at Chivvy Chase.

'What is it, Ali?' asked Miss Copewell.

'That word you spoke, Miss. It's a word my uncle used to use a lot when he was in England. It means "what for" or "why". My uncle was always asking us funny questions which he couldn't answer himself, like "What is beyond space?" or "If a rocket could travel faster than light, would it always be in the dark?" But whenever we asked him "why ?" or "what for?" he would only answer "kyunki" which means "because".'

'Ali's right,' said Mr Browser. 'I remember the words for why and because from the time I was on the North-West Frontier. Where is your uncle now, Ali?'

'He went back to Pakistan, Mr Browser. He wanted to think more, and he said it was too cold in England for him to think properly. We haven't heard of him for a long time.'

Miss Copewell waved impatiently to Mr Browser.

'Never mind all that,' she said. 'The man wants us to go aboard.'

Mr Browser went to the front of the line and introduced himself to an old man in a sailor's cap, who studied the papers Mr Browser handed him and then waved them aboard.

'They can sit themselves anywhere,' he said, 'but there's no need to go below yet. They can come and buy drinks from there later on.'

The boat, it seemed, was run by a crew of two— the old man and his son, Dave.

'Thought I was out of work for the rest of the year,' the old man told Mr Browser, 'then suddenly an Indian gentleman appears and tells me his new River Boat Company can offer me a few trips with this old wreck. I'd have been stupid to turn the offer down, wouldn't I?'

'Yes,' agreed Mr Browser. 'I see the boat's name is freshly painted.'

'Yes, I says to the Indian gent, the boat ought to have a name, and he says, "Call it the *Kiswasti*."

So I says, "How do you spell it?" and he says, "Don't worry about the spelling." So there it is. Dave! Start her up!' He signed to his son, who was at the wheel. 'Fortunately, it's a calm little river,' he went on. 'We shan't go far into the estuary, just take a look and come back. I wouldn't trust this craft for long in the open sea.'

Mr Browser was inclined to agree with him. Loose planks rattled as the class rushed to find the best places to sit, and Spiky Jackson at once found a piece of the handrail which had worked loose, and waggled it about.

'Leave it alone, Simon!' Mr Browser warned him. 'We don't want anyone falling overboard.'

Indeed, this was a nightmare Mr Browser suffered from whenever fate or Mr Sage involved him in trips on the water with children. This one, however, seemed to be turning out a peaceful, danger free voyage. The River Graywater flowed—perhaps crept would be a better word—at a lazy pace toward the open sea, and in places was so narrow that another boat of the same size could not have managed to pass them.

The little lock through which they sailed was so small—Dave and the captain had to operate it themselves—that the class was not greatly impressed.

'Old Browser's drawing on the blackboard was more exciting than that,' declared Martin, and

they gave a cheer when shortly after leaving the
lock behind, the old man announced that drinks
were now available below. Thanks to Miss Copewell and Mr Browser, the scrum for refreshments
was kept in order, and there were no major
mishaps, though Melanie Friar suddenly burst
into tears.

'Stop the boat!' cried her friend Anna. 'Melanie's dropped her purse overboard. Mr Browser,
she's lost all her money. What can we do?'

41

Mr Browser wondered if they hoped he would jump overboard. The old captain made sure he didn't.

'Can't do nothing about that!' he yelled from the wheel. 'Water's black as pitch here—a diver would have his work cut out to find a purse. Silly girl to let it fall in!'

So Melanie cried into her lemonade, and Miss Copewell comforted her and gave her a twenty pence piece.

'There's the sea ahead!' shouted Michael. The little river did its best to broaden out, so that Mr Browser could remind them that rivers widen at their mouths and silt is deposited on the banks. Small waves began to plop against the sides of the *Kiswasti*.

'Shan't go much further,' shouted the old man to his son. 'See that old building over there, you kids? That used to be a lighthouse. Ships would sometimes get stuck on the sandbanks, if their captains didn't know what they were about. Right, Dave, that's it. Hard to port!'

At the very moment he spoke, a wind began to blow up, causing the torn awning to flap noisily, and making the waves foam as they hit the ship.

'Harder, Dave! Turn her around quick—we're moving too fast out to sea!'

'Put the engine full on!' Dave retorted. 'We need more power.'

'It is full on,' declared his father. 'Confound it—we've struck a squall. Better make for the shore!'

Melanie, already upset by the loss of her purse, was ready to panic.

'Help! We're drifting out to sea!' she cried.

'Be quiet, Melanie!' ordered Mr Browser with unusual severity. 'We're doing a little manoeuvring, that's all. Sit down, everyone. We don't want anyone falling over and injuring themselves.'

The children remained seated and kept a somewhat frightened calm, but the behaviour of Dave and the skipper did not help. Their movements were jerky and excited, and they shouted nervously at each other—clearly to little effect. The wind was rising all the time, and now the *Kiswasti* was drifting sideways out to sea.

'When are we going to stop?' shouted Anna.

'Not for a hundred miles, if we keep going in this direction,' Selwyn Jordan replied. 'We'll end up off the coast of Holland, probably.'

Anna turned pale, because she respected the serious Selwyn's knowledge.

'Don't be silly,' said Mr Browser automatically. 'We'll soon be turning back.'

But now few of them believed him. They were now well beyond the point where the old lighthouse stood, heading for the foam-crested waves on the ocean.

'Perhaps we'll be picked up by a liner,' suggested

Spiky. 'Then we'd have to go back to a big port, and we wouldn't be home until late tonight.'

'If we're lucky,' said Selwyn.

'Quiet!' demanded Mr Browser, and couldn't think of anything else to say.

The boat began to toss in the waves, and several faces turned from pale to a greeny shade. Mr Browser struggled to speak to the old captain.

'What are you doing?' he asked. 'Hadn't we better make for the shore?'

'That's what we're trying to do,' the old man shouted back. 'This wind has come from nowhere. We'll have to hope it drops when we're further out.'

This seemed a modest sort of hope to Mr Browser, and he was making his way back to the cowering passengers when the *Kiswasti* lurched and threw him full length on the deck.

'Oh dear, Mr Browser,' cried Miss Copewell, and staggered to his side.

'Hold tight!' yelled Dave. 'We've hit a sandbank!'

The *Kiswasti* was grinding and shuddering, and when Spiky looked over the side he could see a stretch of sand fringed with little crested waves. The boat turned further on its side like an old dog settling down to rest, and the children on one side were flung from their seats and slithered across the deck to join the rest of the party.

'Water coming in below!' shouted Dave, and the skipper took prompt action. He forced open the handrail and shoved the gangplank down to the sand.

'Get them off the boat!' he yelled to Mr Browser. 'She could easily start breaking up, or even tilt right over. The weight of the children is stopping her from righting herself. They'll be safe on the sandbank while Dave and I try to ease her off again. Perhaps you could help too, sir!'

'All right,' agreed Mr Browser, looking suspiciously at the sandbank. He edged down the gangplank and stepped through the shallow water, up to his ankles in sand.

'It's safe,' he called to the anxious Miss Copewell. 'Let them come off one at a time, please.'

So Class 8 disembarked, glad to be off the

creaking boat, but doubtful about the safety of the sandbank.

'Suppose the tide rises?' asked Anna. 'Won't we all be—' She couldn't face saying the rest.

'Don't worry,' called out Dave. 'We have a small dinghy at the back. If necessary we'll row ashore and get help if we can't right the boat. The tide won't be high for another three hours yet.'

'Three hours,' said Anna. 'That's not long.'

'Come with me to the middle of the sandbank,' said Mr Browser. 'It'll be drier there.'

He was disturbed by the knowledge that the tide could be expected to rise for the next three hours, and he had heard plenty about the shifting sands in the estuary. He gathered the class together, and they watched the old man and his son make fruitless efforts to shift the obstinate craft. Mr Browser went to help, but he had come to the conclusion that they would never succeed, and the old man evidently realised it too.

'Wish I'd never met that Indian fellow,' he admitted to Mr Browser. 'Nice chap, he seemed, with a white moustache and beard. Well, we'd better free the dinghy. We don't want that to be smashed.'

They moved to the back of the *Kiswasti*, where a tiny rowing boat was lashed to the stern, and set to work to free it.

'Oh dear,' said Miss Copewell. 'The wind is

46

growing stronger. I do hope the children don't catch cold.'

'Spiky!' whispered Michael.

'Yes?'

'The wind—it's making the same sound as we heard that night—'

He was interrupted by a sharp explosion, and then the wind descended upon them with tremendous power.

'It's a whirlwind!' cried Miss Copewell as the sky suddenly darkened.

'They're coming again!' shouted Spiky, as his friends covered their ears and cowered on the sand. 'Quick, Mike, that thing will come that clawed up the desks. Run!'

He stood up shakily to try and run, but the force of the wind knocked him back, and he was powerless to resist, just like the rest, when the huge, claw-like grab came down upon them, enclosed them in darkness and lifted them away from the sandbank, taking with it some inches of sand. Upset by the wind and the darkness, the old man and his son struggled to hold on to the dinghy, which they had almost freed. When the wind surged upwards instead of downwards, they clung for their lives to the rail of the *Kiswasti*, which was already breaking up under the force of the blast. Gradually the wind died down and the darkness lifted; with relief they realised that the dinghy and its oars were undamaged, and pulled it free from the *Kiswasti*.

'Done it!' cried the old man, and turned to reassure Mr Browser and the children. 'We'll soon bring help—' he began, but the words died in his throat as he stared at the lifeless sandbank.

'Come on, Dad,' said Dave, 'we'd better carry it further away—the *Kiswasti* is breaking up fast.'

'Dave!' shouted the old man. 'They're gone! Dave—where are those kids?'

Dave put the dinghy down on the sand and stared in horror. Then he ran like a madman to the centre of the sandbank. 'Where are you?' he cried. 'Come back, wherever you've gone!'

His only answer was the plopping of the little waves on the sand. The old man joined him.

'Vanished,' he muttered. 'Gone in a flash.'

Dave stamped on the sand.

'They can't have sunk into the sand,' he said. 'It's firm enough.'

'Maybe the wind blew them into the water.'

They searched along the edge of the sandbank, but there was no sign of a single child.

'Look—a shoe!' cried Dave suddenly, and dashed into the water. He came back with a girl's red shoe in his hand, the only evidence that Class 8 had ever existed.

A creaking and cracking noise diverted their attention from the shoe. Turning, they saw the *Kiswasti* shifting and sinking on her side, the

48

old timbers snapping and crumbling.

'Shifting sands!' whispered the old man. 'We can't stay here any longer, Dave. We must get ashore and report. Oh, those poor children!'

They pushed the dinghy into the water and struck out for the shore. With the wind dropping and the incoming tide to help them, a quarter of an hour's hard rowing brought them to a deserted part of the marshy shore. They scrambled out and pulled the dinghy on land after them.

'We must find a phone,' said the old man shakily. 'Dial 999. Though what can they do—'

Dave was not listening to him. He was gazing out to sea, where not a single ship was to be seen. The *Kiswasti,* overcome by sea and sand, had broken up and disappeared from sight.

4

The Kingdom of the Kiswastis

Mr Browser was too busy trying to keep his spectacles on his nose to be able to do much to help the screaming members of Class 8. They were all being tossed about like peas being shaken in a bowl, and the darkness inside the giant grab made the experience more frightening.

Gradually the movement of their container became steadier, and the bodies settled at the bottom as the peas would do when the bowl is put down on the table. They disentangled themselves, grateful to find they were still alive.

'We haven't been drowned, have we?' called out Anna.

''Course not,' answered Selwyn. 'We can breathe all right.'

'That doesn't mean that we're above water level,' said Martin gloomily.

'The thing came from above us and scooped us up,' said Spiky. 'It took some sand, too. I can feel it underneath me.'

'You're right,' agreed Anna, but wasn't comforted for long. 'Are we in the mouth of some horrible sea monster?'

'Don't be silly, Anna,' said Miss Copewell.

'Then you tell me where we are!' suggested Anna

51

sulkily, and Miss Copewell was silent, for of course she hadn't the slightest idea where she was, nor of her destination.

'We must keep calm,' said Mr Browser, asserting himself. 'Is everyone all right? Nobody hurt?'

'I think I've twisted my ankle,' said Michael.

'If that's all,' declared Mr Browser, 'we can count ourselves lucky. We must be on the way somewhere.'

'What in?' asked Selwyn bluntly. 'This isn't part of our trip, is it Mr Browser?'

'Of course not.'

'I think I've seen this thing we're in before,' announced Spiky. 'Or something very like it. So has Michael.'

'Seen it before? Surely that's not possible, Simon!'

'Yes, Mr Browser. It came down one night and took away all the old desks, and then it came again and took some chairs and other things from Mr Watchett's shed. I think there were pencils, chalk, a blackboard—and several other things which have been missing.'

'What on earth—' began Mr Browser.

'I think he must have hit himself on the head,' suggested Miss Copewell. 'Just keep quiet and stop worrying, Simon dear. Everything will be all right soon.'

'But he's right!' put in Michael. 'We did see a

huge, claw-like thing take the chairs away. It's all true!'

Mr Browser was growing more and more irritated.

'What is all this nonsense!' he demanded. 'If you saw this thing at school, why didn't anyone else see it?'

'Mr Watchett did,' said Spiky. 'It was at seven o'clock at night, that's why no one else was there.'

'But surely Mr Watchett would have told somebody, especially if the chairs and desks were taken.'

'He put them there for the thing to take,' explained Spiky.

'Yes, and he was too afraid to say anything in case he was captured himself,' added Michael. 'I think he was under a sort of spell. He made us promise not to tell anyone what we had seen.'

'And now we're the captives!' concluded Spiky.

Anna started to cry.

'But who would want old desks and pencils and chalks—and us?' she sobbed. Mr Browser couldn't answer that one, but he did his best.

'There looks to be some purpose in all of this,' he said. 'We can only lie here and wait to find out what it is.'

'It's growing very stuffy in here,' observed Miss Copewell. 'I suggest that we all stop talking and just lie quietly, so that we don't use up more

53

oxygen than is necessary. I don't see any windows anywhere.'

Her words had a chilling effect on the party, and they obeyed fearfully. In the silence, there was nothing to be heard outside, however hard they listened. The grab, if it were moving, did so in uncanny quietness. The children and Miss Copewell wished they had never come on the trip, and Mr Browser blamed Mr Sage for persuading him to arrange it—but it was no good grumbling. He looked at the luminous dial of his watch. They had been travelling for five minutes in the grab, yet it seemed like hours.

Gradually, though, the fears and discomforts of the children died away, and Mr Browser himself was overcome by a pleasant drowsiness. The grab was shooting upwards like a lift which has forgotten to stop, carrying its semi-conscious load out of the Earth's atmosphere and into the realms of space, where it homed in to its mother craft. The grab moved above the craft, settled into position on its roof, and waited. Slowly, part of the roof of the bigger craft slid to one side, leaving the grab perched over a large gap. To the sound of a slight humming the claws of the grab began to move, and it tilted to one side. Soon the jaws were open wide enough for the nearest child—Michael Fairlie—to roll into the gap and float gently down to the floor of the area below. As the jaws parted, so more and

more children were tipped out of the grab, like
sweets being emptied from a large jar. Their
descent to the floor was steady, and they floated
down in the style of a swimmer allowing himself to
sink beneath the surface of the water. The floor of
the area was soft, as if covered by a large, wall to
wall mattress. Unlike the grab, the room was air-
conditioned, and the new occupants passed from
unhealthy unconsciousness into a pleasant sleep.
The roof slid silently back into place, and the craft,
with the grab still attached, streamed at a speed
undreamt of on Earth through millions of miles of
space.

Before it reached its destination the captives awoke one by one, most of them surprised not to find themselves in their own beds at home.

'Spiky!' whispered Michael, crawling across to his friend. 'We've been kidnapped by that thing! But it seems much more comfortable now.'

Spiky sat up and stared in dismay at the bare walls of the room, which appeared to contain no doors nor windows.

'This isn't the thing that grabbed us,' he decided. 'It was dark in there—I can remember what happened now. We were all thrown in on top of one another, and I could hardly breathe. We must have been transferred somewhere else. Mr Browser—wake up! Where are we?'

'Yes, Mr Browser,' piped up Anna. 'It's very comfortable here—like a giant trampoline—but I'd like to know where we're going.'

She sprang into the air several times off the mattress-like base to demonstrate what she meant.

'Yes, Mr Browser—tell us!' joined in several other voices. Mr Browser propped himself up on his elbow and adjusted his glasses nervously. He was very concerned at the trust which they placed in him, but he decided he had better be honest.

'I really haven't a clue where we are or what is our destination,' he admitted, 'but I must say that I'm pleased to be alive after that unfortunate experience on the sandbank.'

'So am I,' put in Miss Copewell. 'We must try and make the best of it. We must be bound for somewhere.'

Selwyn Jordan cast a look of pity at Miss Copewell.

'You have no idea, Miss,' he said solemnly, 'of what may have happened to us. I don't suppose you've ever thought that one day you might end up in outer space?'

'Not really, Selwyn,' said Miss Copewell, smoothing her skirt. 'I prefer to think we are being taken home in some sort of luxury liner—'

'What a hope!' said Anna Cardwell, and did a somersault on the mattress to show her contempt for Miss Copewell's idea. 'We're captured,' she went on when she was the right way up again. 'Have you ever seen a cabin on a liner without any portholes or doors?'

Miss Copewell hadn't, and she was at a loss for something to say. Mr Browser tried to calm her.

'We must have been preserved for some purpose,' he declared. 'All we have to do is wait and see what it is.'

'It's my birthday at the end of next week,' observed Spiky. 'I hope we don't have to wait too long.'

'Oh, I'm sure we'll be home by then,' said Miss Copewell, trying to follow the example of Mr Browser's cheerfulness. But her attempt had the

opposite effect.

'I don't see how we can be,' said Michael, and little Ali Khan spoke up from the corner.

'I feel we are very far away from home,' he said. 'I feel it in my bones. My mother said only last week that strange things were happening. She said she saw a vision of my uncle in the High Street of Chivvy Chase when she went shopping, yet he is supposed to be in Pakistan. Now there is this boat called *Kiswasti* and —'

'What does your uncle look like?' asked Mr Browser, glad to be able to change the subject.

'He has a white beard and moustache, and little

twinkling eyes,' said Ali Khan. 'But sometimes his eyes seem to stand still, when he looks far away as though you weren't there. That's when he's thinking.'

'Strange,' said Mr Browser. 'The captain of the *Kiswasti* said an Indian of that description told him to call the boat by that name. I suppose he wouldn't know the difference between a Pakistani and an Indian.'

'It was my uncle!' said Ali Khan. 'Perhaps it was no vision my mother saw. What is he doing here, that strange man?'

'Oh, I don't suppose it was him,' said Mr Browser, seeing this line of conversation had led to more anxiety for Ali.

'I bet we're not back for my birthday,' said Spiky.

'If ever,' said Anna.

'Quiet!' ordered Mr Browser. 'This won't do any good at all. I forbid anyone to say any more about where we're going. Has anyone any sweets?'

Hands went up, and paper bags were produced from pockets.

'We must share them out,' said Mr Browser, 'so that everyone has something to eat. Let's put them all together in one pile, and Miss Copewell and I will give them out.'

This was not popular with those who had bought sweets on the boat and had plenty left, but in the end all were handed over. Dividing out the sweets helped to pass the time, which had been Mr Browser's chief object. Soon all the children were lying back chewing or sucking happily, with the knowledge that there were still two more sweets each to come.

'Maybe we aren't going anywhere at all,' suggested Spiky. 'Maybe we've already arrived!'

Their curiosity was not to be satisfied until after two half-hourly distributions of sweets had been made by Mr Browser. The last of these sweets had been eaten when those members of the class who were not dozing could see that the roof above them was slowly splitting in the middle, the halves sliding away to left and right and leaving a gap in the middle. Fascinated, they watched as a kind of ladder with a platform on it descended from the gap, stopping with the platform halfway to the floor.

'Maybe they want us to climb up there,' said Anna anxiously.

'They'll have to bring the ladder down further if they want that,' declared Selwyn. 'We can't jump so high.'

Anna's suggestion was proved wrong when a man appeared at the top of the ladder and slowly started to descend. When he reached the platform, he turned round and sat down cross legged on it. The children saw on old, dark skinned man with a white beard and moustache, and wrinkles on his forehead, who looked down at them out of twinkling blue eyes. He was wearing what Spiky termed simply a white sheet and a kind of scarf wound around his head.

The silence caused by this gentleman's arrival was unexpectedly broken by Ali Khan. He suddenly spoke up in a language strange to all the rest, who turned away from the newcomer to look at the excited face of Ali. When Ali finished speaking, they turned back to the stranger, who answered in the same language as Ali had used. Ali then stood up and made a little bow to the stranger. Spiky could contain his curiosity no longer.

'Tell us what it's all about, Ali,' he demanded. 'Is he a friend of yours?'

'He is my uncle,' replied Ali. 'He is going to tell us why we are here.'

'That won't help much,' said Spiky. 'You'll have to translate for us.'

'No, no—that won't be necessary. My uncle lived with us in England for some time before he returned to Pakistan in order to meditate.'

'Meditate?'

'That means think,' explained Anna. 'Are we in Pakistan, then?'

The white bearded gentleman laughed.

'He speaks good English,' said Ali. 'I am sure he will tell us all we need to know.'

61

The little old man nodded and smiled at them.

'My nephew has spoken the truth,' he said, speaking with only the slightest of accents. 'I fear that it is because of me that you are all here, though I did not intend it to happen—'

'Please come to the point, sir,' asked Mr Browser politely but firmly. 'How can you be responsible for what has happened to us?'

'If you will kindly listen,' replied the old man, 'all will be made clear to you.'

'Please go ahead.'

'But I must start at the beginning, or you may not understand. As Ali has told you, I came to England with his father and mother years ago, but the weather did not suit me. I was covered with aches and pains, and also I was not happy at my work, and could find no peace. So I decided to return to Pakistan, to spend the rest of my life in working on my brother's land and in thinking about the world and the universe of which the world is part. In Pakistan there is much more time for thinking; you can sit on a warm evening and send your thoughts up to the stars in the Milky Way. You can see the stars so much more clearly there, and because of that your thoughts seem clearer, too.'

Mr Browser coughed and stirred impatiently.

'There, you see,' said the old man, smiling. 'You are all in so much hurry, where you come from.

63

You so much want to enjoy your lives, that you hardly have time for work, let alone thinking.'

'Where is all this leading?' demanded Miss Copewell huffily. 'Surely we haven't been brought here to listen to you talking?'

'Indeed not, madam,' said the old man politely. 'It brings us to this: one night while I was meditating in a field on my brother's land, I made contact with another world. Yes, my thoughts had reached out into space, further than the cleverest rockets have travelled.'

He was proud enough to pause at this moment, which gave Anna Cardwell the chance to speak.

'How do you know all this?'

'I know, my child, because several days later, just after dusk had fallen, I was thinking in the same field when a kind of giant claw came down upon me and snatched me up. I was carried away and brought to the very world with which I had made contact in my thoughts.'

'That's the same claw that grabbed us!' said Spiky. 'So we're on our way to this other world too!'

'Exactly, my boy. In fact, you are nearly there. I have been sent on this craft to prepare you for your arrival.'

'But why have they chosen us?' asked Anna.

'It's probably my fault,' admitted the old man. 'They are very keen to learn all about our world, and I talked to them at first in Urdu, the common language of our continent, and told them about my own country. We talked by means of a machine—a kind of computer which is able to act as an interpreter. I talked for hours into the machine, and it learned how to unscramble my words and report what I had said to them. They communicate often by means of a little machine attached to the hand. It responds to the slightest finger movement, and the fingers of these people are very delicate and sensitive. Soon they wanted to know about the rest of the world, and which is the most widely used language, so I told them about English, and that my nephew lived in England and was learning quickly in an English school. They were curious about this, because they have no schools in their world, as there is so very little to learn. Their world is a completely boring one. Their food comes chiefly from a kind of grasslike crop, which they process and eat in pill form. There is only one kind of tree, one type of bird, no real hills and only one kind of flower. They have enough to live on, but very little to do, and so they have concentrated all their curiosity on the exploration of other worlds. They built a vast complex called "The Museum of Other Worlds", and in it they have put rocks and soil brought from the other worlds their space craft have reached. Unfortunately, these other worlds seem to have been more boring than their own, and when they discovered ours, with its great variety of scenery and things to do, you can imagine how excited they were. They worked until they had invented a space craft which could orbit the Earth and bring back samples for them to study. I was the first sample they brought back, because it was through my thoughts that they first contacted the Earth. You are the second sample—a sample which will help them to learn the English language and to find out about the way children live on Earth.'

'You mean we're here for them to study?' asked Mr Browser.

'Precisely,' agreed the old man.

'Then we're just like the newts and stick insects that we take to school,' said Anna.

'Sort of,' he admitted.

'How long are we supposed to be here for?' demanded Spiky after they had taken this information in.

'That I do not know,' admitted the old man with a frown. 'They haven't said anything to me about arrangements for a return journey.'

'I wish you hadn't told them about us, Uncle,' said Ali Khan sadly.

'I am sorry, my boy. They were so interested in the wonderful English education system that I was carried away. If I had only known—'

'What are these people called?' asked Selwyn

Jordan, who always liked to have everything labelled so that he could remember the names. This brought mutterings of 'Who cares?' from Spiky and others. The old man smiled.

'I asked them that, and their reply was not very clear. It sounded a bit like an Urdu word, so I called them the Kiswastis.'

'The name of the boat we sailed on,' said Anna.

'Yes. I gave it that name.'

'So it was all planned,' said Michael, 'just like the taking of the desks and chairs. Shall we be seeing them too?'

'Yes indeed, later on. You will first be given accommodation, and then you will go to the Museum of Other Worlds, where you will find your classroom reconstructed as near as possible.'

'So we'll be specimens in a museum!' called out Anna, looking ready to burst into tears.

'That's right!' said the old man, and suddenly the ladder with its platform was drawn up again to the roof. The old man disappeared, and the gap in the roof slowly closed.

The human specimens were once more enclosed in their doorless, windowless room, prisoners of the as yet unknown Kiswastis.

5

Mr Watchett Speaks Up

When the old sailor and his son Dave had convinced themselves that there was nothing of the *Kiswasti* left in sight, they set off across the marshes as quickly as they could in the direction of the nearest house. The barking of his dog brought the farmer out to meet them, and he listened as they poured out their story, the old man panting and gasping for breath, and both of them, judged the farmer, still suffering from shock.

So he called the police for them and invited them in for a cup of tea. The police rang the nearest lifeboat station along the coast, and then, to be sure this was no hoax, also tried to contact the River Boat Company to find out if the *Kiswasti* had been hired to a school. Here they drew blank; the offices of the River Boat Company appeared to be closed, or no one was answering the phone. Then they rang Mr Sage at Chivvy Chase School.

'Could you please confirm that a party from your school has gone on a trip down the River Graywater in a boat called the *Kiswasti*?'

'That's correct,' said Mr Sage, and his heart began to sink. 'Why—what have they been up to?' he asked, pretending cheerfulness.

'I'm afraid, sir, that the boat has been reported missing,' said the inspector, the gravity in his voice squashing completely Mr Sage's attempt to treat the affair lightheartedly.

'Missing? How can that be? Surely no boat can go missing on the River Graywater!'

'No, sir, but it seems that the boat ventured into the estuary, where a sudden storm carried it on to a sandbank, where it broke up. The children could still be on the sandbank—a lifeboat is on its way already—but I must warn you that the captain reports no sign of life from the shore.'

'Oh no!' cried Mr Sage, banging his fist on the

table in despair. 'I should have known better. Class 8 again—'

'Don't blame yourself, sir,' said the policeman automatically.

'What can we do?' begged Mr Sage.

'Only have a list of those on the trip ready for the local police when they call round—and also have any letters from the River Boat Company available. We are trying to establish contact with them now.'

Mr Sage collapsed in his chair.

'Miss Copewell!' he called, and then he remembered that Miss Copewell had gone on the trip with Class 8, and he gave an extra little groan before he called Mrs Crisp the Welfare Assistant to help him prepare the list.

'Oh dear, Class 8,' said Mrs Crisp, shaking her head as though she possessed some knowledge denied to Mr Sage. 'They're so accident prone! Poor Miss Copewell!'

'Yes, indeed,' said Mr Sage, and stared at the wall in front of him without finding any comfort in the pictures of the staff, the school football team or the school netball team.

'I shouldn't have let them go!' he muttered as Mrs Crisp left to copy out the list and make an extra cup of tea. 'Browser seems to invite trouble, wherever he goes!'

While Mr Sage was bemoaning his fate, the

police were knocking on the doors of the offices of the River Boat Company, which were in a little flat above a fish and chip shop. Nobody answered, and at last the door was broken down. All the police found were empty filing cabinets and dirty cups and saucers; the owners of the River Boat Company had flown.

The lifeboat, manned by volunteers from the little seaside town of Rocksea, arrived in the area described, and found that parts of a large, shifting sandbank were still to be seen above the rising tide. The boat came as near to the sand as it could in the shallow water, and the skipper studied the sand through a strong pair of binoculars.

'Bits of wood and something else on the far side, Joe,' he called out. 'Better go over and check it.'

Joe, the youngest member of the crew, swung himself over the side and splashed through the water in his thigh length waterboots, while the rest of the crew discussed the grim fate of the *Kiswasti*.

'Broken her back and sucked under by a current, I reckon,' said one. 'Maybe bits of her will turn up somewhere along the coast, but who's to say when or where?'

'Some of her may be already beneath the sand,' was the opinion of the oldest member. 'Gone to join the hundreds of other wooden ships that have disappeared off this shore.'

Joe came back, and his face was ashen grey. He

held up two bits of plank in one hand, and in the other a bar of chocolate in an orange coloured wrapper.

'That's all there is, mates!' he said, and the crew stared at the hateful water frothing over the slimy sand. Just as the captain had started the engine up again, they were joined by a police launch which had come down the river.

'Any sign?' called a policeman through a loud hailer.

'Only these,' answered the skipper, and Joe held up what he had found. Both boats returned to base, and the police faced up to the dreaded task of informing Mr Sage and the parents concerned of the disappearance of their children.

'Mr Watchett,' said Mr Sage when he had heard the news, 'put some chairs in the hall. When the parents come to collect their children I shall ask them to go to the hall and I'll break the news to them there. A policeman and a policewoman will be there as well.'

'Yes, Mr Sage. All Class 8, did you say? It don't seem possible, Mr Sage. On the River Graywater? I've been fishing there often, and it's so calm you could hear the fish flipping their fins. Incredible, Mr Sage.'

'Yes, I can't understand it either,' agreed Mr Sage.

'That boy Simon Jackson and his friend Mi-

chael something—'

'Michael Fairlie.'

'That's him. They're both in that class, aren't they?'

'They are,' said Mr Sage, as if in a dream. Mr Watchett went about his work without his usual unruffled calm. He frowned and shook his head from time to time as he set all the chairs out for the parents.

'I daren't tell!' he muttered once. 'I just daren't!'

The parents, who as usual were gathering at the school gate as they did when waiting the return of a party on an outing, were none too pleased when Mr Sage invited them to come into school, where he had something to tell them.

'Tell us now!' said Mrs Cardwell. 'I don't want to hang about—I've a youngster at home, and I can't leave him for long—'

But when Mr Sage refused and gravely insisted that they meet in the hall, and when they saw a police car on the premises, they silently obeyed. In the hall the presence of the policeman and the policewoman filled them with foreboding. When parents of twenty out of the thirty missing children were seated, Mr Sage rose to speak. Mr Watchett stood at the back of the hall, as if ready to bring more chairs if they were needed.

'I very much regret,' announced Mr Sage quietly, 'that there has been an accident to the boat on which Class 8 were making their trip down the river. At the moment, we have no news of them, but we are in constant touch with the police, who will inform us as soon as anything is heard. The disappearance of the boat—'

'Disappearance!' cried Mrs Cardwell. 'The whole boat has disappeared—is that what you're telling me?'

'I am afraid so,' admitted Mr Sage, and prepared himself to face the very worst moments of his life. He was wishing he could run out of the door and out of the school, for the white faces of the amazed parents were beginning to react to his announcement—when suddenly there came an unexpected interruption.

'Ladies!' shouted Mr Watchett from the back of the hall. 'I don't believe your children are drowned. I think they could still be alive, but where, I cannot say.'

All heads were turned towards Mr Watchett, and the policeman walked across to him as if he believed the caretaker had gone out of his mind.

'Explain yourself, Mr Watchett,' said Mr Sage, who suspected that this interruption would only cause a few moments of delay before the storm broke. Mr Watchett, usually very shy of speaking in public, a man who liked to keep himself to himself, strode forward without hesitation, so that the advancing policeman stopped and allowed

75

him to pass.

'Strange things have been happening at this school,' began the caretaker. 'Things over which I have no control.'

Mr Watchett spoke as though he had control over everything which usually took place at Chivvy Chase, and Mr Sage frowned.

'What things?' he asked bluntly.

'Desks have been taken, and then chairs,' explained Mr Watchett, 'as well as some classroom materials which teachers have missed lately.'

'What has this to do with our children?' called out Mrs Cardwell impatiently.

'I'm coming to it, lady,' went on the caretaker calmly. 'These things have all been taken by some mysterious force, a giant claw-like container which came down and grabbed them away. I must have been under the power of this thing, because I put the chairs and the desks outside the shed for them to be taken. The second time, two boys from Mr Browser's class came home across the field after dark, and they saw what happened. That's why I am wondering whether they have been taken up in this—thing too!'

'Where did it go?' asked the policeman, as if to humour Mr Watchett, who, he still thought, must be deranged.

'Upwards,' said the caretaker, raising both arms in a gesture of helplessness. 'There was a strong

wind, and some dust—I couldn't really see.'

'Why was this not reported to me?' demanded Mr Sage angrily.

'I told you,' said Mr Watchett. 'I was under the influence of these creatures, whoever they are, and I felt in my bones that if I talked I might be snatched away too!'

'Under the influence,' wrote the policeman in his notebook.

'You don't believe me!' cried out the caretaker excitedly, 'but I'm offering these people the only hope that their children are still alive. If I'm wrong, then the situation is far worse, isn't it?'

Mr Sage was bound to agree, and for the rest of the meeting everything was done to try to comfort the heartbroken parents, most of whom attached little importance at all to Mr Watchett's story, and pinned their slender hopes on the return of the *Kiswasti*.

They were promised by Mr Sage and the police that they would be informed instantly if any news were to come through, and shuffled away from the meeting as if stunned. Most of them spoke little or not at all, but Mrs Cardwell, like her daughter, was never at a loss for words.

'This is the last straw,' she declared. 'I've always thought it a funny old school, and now it seems the caretaker is crazy too. I shall send Anna away—'

Here she realised the grim possibilities again, and stopped to dab her eyes with her handkerchief.

'I shall take her away if she comes back,' she sobbed.

Meanwhile Mr Watchett was showing Mr Sage and the police the shed from which the desks and chairs had vanished.

'How is it,' asked the policeman, 'that you've been able to conquer your fears and speak about what you claim has happened?'

'Because I have a hunch,' said the caretaker,

'that it's not me they're after, but a whole class of children. They've taken enough desks and chairs and paints and things for a whole class. My fears have died away—I don't think they want any more—yet.'

'Equipment for one class,' wrote the policeman, because there was nothing else he could do or write about the case. No crime is more difficult to prove than when the bodies vanish completely.

'I do hope they turn up,' he said to Mr Sage. 'Alive, I mean.'

'So do I,' echoed Mr Sage, and promised himself that if they did he would never send Mr Browser down the river with a class again.

6

The Museum of Other Worlds

The journey to the planet of the Kiswastis took another two Earth hours; the craft landed without the slightest vibration, and the passengers would not have known they had arrived if the gap in the roof had not opened again and the ladder been let down, this time to floor level. The old man peered down at them from above.

'The flight is completed,' he told them. 'You can climb up the ladder and you will be taken to your quarters.'

Mr Browser automatically arranged the class in line, then climbed up the ladder himself first. When they emerged from the craft they were directed by Ali's uncle along a corridor with transparent walls.

'Look!' whispered Michael to Spiky. 'I've seen that before!'

Lying on the ground outside the corridor, in a huge square surrounded by buildings, was the giant grab which had seized first the desks, then the chairs—and now the whole of Mr Browser's class.

'It's huge!' said Spiky. 'It could almost have lifted up the whole ship.' The jaws of the grab were open, and some small figures were busy inside and

80

around it.

'They're cleaning it after the flight,' guessed
Michael. 'It must have grabbed up quite a lot of
sand with us.'

Before they reached the end of the corridor they
met their first Kiswastis, who came forward to
receive them. They were short, stocky creatures
with dark, fuzzy hair and watery, pale skins.

'What a hairy lot!' whispered Spiky, noticing
the hairs sprouting from their ears and the furry
growth on the backs of their hands.

'They all look alike!' said Michael. 'What are
they wearing those head covers for?'

'That is to protect them against possible infection from viruses,' explained Ali's uncle. 'You are freshly come from Earth, and you may be carrying infections with you.'

'That's an insult!' commented Anna staring at the Kiswastis in their transparent helmets.

The Kiswastis took over from the old man and led the party out of a door at the end of a corridor, across the wide open space in which the grab was being serviced, and into a dome-shaped building on the other side of it. Beyond that they caught a glimpse of a huge dome of similar shape which dwarfed the first one into which they were being led. They assembled in an entrance hall, and Ali's uncle was called upon to speak by the Kiswastis.

'I shall soon be leaving you,' he explained, 'as I have other duties to perform. I have been teaching this group of Kiswastis some English. They will speak with slight Eastern accent, yes? But you will understand them. Your accommodation is in this building. You will be given food and will be allowed to relax for the rest of the day. The Kiswasti night lasts six Earth hours and never changes—here there is no summer, autumn, winter or spring. Time goes on without division into months or years, and the climate never varies. Every seven days there is a fall of rain, produced by Kiswasti scientists, otherwise it is dry and cloudless. Clouds are formed on the night of the

82

sixth day, and are ready to break into rain at exactly the same time each seventh day. So the Kiswastis do have a period similar to what we call a week.'

'How boring!' called out Anna.

'Exactly,' agreed Ali's uncle. 'The planet of the Kiswastis is so boring, as I have told you, that you are here to provide them with something interesting to watch. After you have rested and slept tonight, you will be taken to the Museum of Other Worlds, where you will continue your lessons as usual.'

'What!' cried Mr Browser. 'Who's going to teach them?'

'You will, of course,' replied the old man, amused. 'You are their teacher, aren't you?'

'Why, yes—but books, and pencils, and all the rest of the materials, what about those? I can't teach properly without them.'

'Don't worry. You will find most things you require in the museum classroom. And now I must really depart. Two more classes of English come to me today. I am sure you will find everything very comfortable, children. Goodbye, Ali— goodbye to all of you.'

The Kiswastis, who were becoming impatient with the old man's wordiness, quickly ushered the children to their rooms. The boys and Mr Browser were all to sleep in one large room, and Miss

Copewell and the girls in one exactly similar opposite them.

There were a number of small cupboards in which clothes could be placed, but little else.

'Where are the beds?' demanded Spiky, and Mr Browser repeated the question politely.

'Bed? Bed on floor,' answered one of the Kiswastis after puzzling out what was meant. As on the space craft, the floor was as soft and springy as a mattress, so this news was not too upsetting.

'But there aren't any pillows,' objected Selwyn. 'I can't sleep properly without a pillow.'

The word 'pillow' was unknown to the attendant Kiswastis, and all attempts to enlighten them had little success. Evidently the Kiswastis were not in the habit of resting their heads on pillows when they slept.

'We'll have to fold up our clothes to make pillows,' Mr Browser suggested in the end, and the Kiswastis prepared to withdraw.

'Food in a short time,' announced one of them as they left. 'Prepared in English way—on plates, and with knife and fork.'

Making polite bows, they retreated, grey little figures in short tunics and trousers buttoned at the ankles.

'They remind me of the Chinese Army,' said Selwyn.

'It's not the plate, knife and fork part of it I'm

worried about,' remarked Martin Portland-Smythe. 'It's the actual food—whether I can eat it.'

Ten minutes later they were led into a dining room which seemed to have been modelled on school or works canteens, and to their relief the food was reasonably tasty. It consisted of a first course made up of a kind of beef and a vegetable with something of potato and something of carrot about it, followed by some black berries which were a cross between raspberries and blackberries.

'I can exist on this,' declared Spiky.

'That is good,' said one of the Kiswastis who had been brought in to report if there were any complaints, 'because this is going to be your menu, with only slight changes, for as long as you are here.'

Soon after the meal they were overcome by sleepiness, and lay down to rest on their huge, communal mattress.

'Wish they'd turn the lights off,' said Anna to Miss Copewell. She need not have worried, for soon the natural light began to fade, and the Kiswastian twilight began. It lasted only thirty seconds, after which everything was in darkness.

The night was short, and the sudden sunrise quickly brought them to life again. Breakfast consisted of the same vegetable, fried this time, and a block of ice water tinged with the taste of the same kind of berries they had eaten on the day before.

'Not very exciting,' was Selwyn's comment.

'Well, they told us it's a boring planet—I suppose boring food is all part of it,' said Spiky.

After breakfast they were lined up by Mr Browser and followed a Kiswasti along a corridor which joined the smaller dome to the huge one. Now and again they crossed intersecting passages, and looking along these they glimpsed sets of stairs which appeared to lead towards the roof of the dome.

Suddenly the tunnel was flooded with light, and they emerged into a huge arena.

'This is bigger than Wembley!' said Spiky.

'Reminds me of Olympia, where they hold those exhibitions,' said Selwyn. 'My mum took me there once. They had houses and shops and all sorts inside, all under one roof.'

'This is ten times bigger than that,' declared Anna. 'And there must be seats for thousands. Look up there!'

The arena was surrounded with seating which reached right up to the transparent roof. The seats were so far away from the ground that each seat was provided with what looked like an oblong kind of telescope.

'Look in the middle!' called out Michael. 'It's a classroom a bit like those at Chivvy Chase!'

'Those are the old chairs and desks,' revealed Spiky. 'Looks as though they've been cleaned and repaired. And piles of our books on the shelves. They've made it up to look something like our classroom!'

They fell silent as the leading Kiswasti took Mr Browser to the centre of the arena and let him in through the transparent door of the classroom, which was also fitted, they discovered as they went in, with equally transparent walls. Miss Copewell brought up the rear, clucking with surprise to see something which resembled her old school surroundings.

'Well, well, well,' she said, 'they've even brought writing books and drawing paper—and there are the missing blackboard compasses. Oh, Mr Browser will be pleased when he hears that we've found them!'

The Kiswasti showed Mr Browser to his place, which was at a table beside an old blackboard and easel.

'Let the class sit as they usually do,' suggested the Kiswasti, and the class found their places.

'The first performance will be in three hours' time,' announced the Kiswasti, 'but we felt that you would like to have a little practice in order to accustom yourselves to your surroundings.'

'Performance!' muttered Mr Browser. 'I'm not one of those teachers who likes to perform, and I don't intend to start now.'

'All that you do will be of great interest to the

Kiswastis,' their guide informed him. 'They have never seen a school in action before.'

'What shall I do?' asked Miss Copewell, and the Kiswasti looked irritated. Miss Copewell's presence on the trip was something they hadn't reckoned with.

'You will sit in this little compartment,' he said, pushing her into a box-like addition to the classroom. 'There will be little to do, because we don't need any forms to be filled in—but you can give out books and help if the children are in any trouble. Now, Mr Browser, perhaps you would like to teach a lesson in your usual manner.'

With a polite little bow the Kiswasti left the classroom. Looking up and around him, Mr Browser could see that there were a number of watchers stationed at various points in the arena, no doubt checking on sound and vision, and making sure that all would be well for the coming show. He stared at the class, and the children stared back at him.

'Well—er, we may as well do something,' he said. 'Selwyn, give out the exercise books—the ones with the thin spaces, for maths. And Anna, while he's doing that, we'll test the acoustics here. Please stand up and say the nine times table.'

'Test the what, Mr Browser?' asked Anna, using her well-known delaying tactics, perfected for maths lessons.

'Acoustics, Anna. I mean you to test the quality of the sound in here.'

'But the—nine times, Mr Browser? I couldn't do that in front of thousands of people, or creatures, or whatever these Kiswastis are—'

'But there aren't thousands of people here, Anna.'

'She can't do it anyway!' jibed Spiky.

'I can!' responded Anna.

'Well, while you're saying it I'll just check on the books we have for our use. Hm—*Maths Comes Alive, English in Stages, Heroes from History* and *Work in the British Isles*. Not what I'd have chosen myself, perhaps, but good, solid stuff. And plenty of stories for you to read. I suppose we can last out for a while with these. Selwyn, give out the *Maths Comes Alive* books. Turn to page ten, and we'll go over our simple addition of fractions. Well done, Anna. You may sit down. Ah—here's a box of pencils. Pass them round, Michael, and be careful they don't break. I only have my old penknife to sharpen them with.'

There's nothing like maths, for bringing people down to earth, and Class 8 could hardly believe Earth had been left behind as they worked away at their earthly sums. The Kiswasti officials watched curiously and used their zoom lenses so that they could try and follow what the children were doing. Soon they grasped what was going on, though one who inspected Spiky's book at close range became very confused and had to move on to other books before the truth dawned.

Mr Browser followed the maths with some English and a talk about Kent, the Garden of England. At this point the concentration of his class waned. Reading and talking about Kent made them realise how far they were from home, and Mr Browser was relieved when the Kiswasti official came back and told him they could break off for a rest and a meal.

'See that you all return fresh and ready to learn,' he told them. 'This afternoon you will be watched by about thirty thousand Kiswastis. You must be prepared to work hard.'

'I shall just be as I usually am,' declared Anna rebelliously. 'Why should I care what these furry creatures think?'

The Kiswasti frowned at her, and Miss Copewell tried to apologise.

'You must do your best in order not to let down Chivvy Chase School, your country and the world,' she told Anna.

'What difference does that make, when we're told we're millions of miles away?' said Anna, suddenly turning tearful. 'Nobody on Earth will know what we're doing, and maybe we'll never see Chivvy Chase School again!'

Miss Copewell thought hard.

'Try your best for Mr Browser and for me,' she said, and Anna just sobbed into her handkerchief.

After the children had been given a meal exactly the same as the one they had eaten the day before, and had had time to rest or amuse themselves, the Kiswastis appeared and told them to make their way back to the arena.

'Thirty thousand Kiswastis, who have travelled from all over our planet, are on their way to watch you during this session; I hope it will be an interesting lesson,' said one of them.

Mr Browser frowned, but said nothing. On the whole he didn't much like people who suggested that his lessons might be made more interesting, whether they were Kiswastis or humans. When the class entered the arena the atmosphere was completely different from that which they had experienced in the morning. A hum of Kiswasti excitement spread all around, and thousands of box-like telescopes were lined up on the faces of Class 8.

'This reminds me of coming out on the pitch at Wembley for a Cup Final,' decided Spiky.

'Oh yes? Which Cup Final were you in?' Anna taunted him.

'You know what I mean,' he muttered. They entered the classroom, where they were protected from any noise the spectators were making. Mr Browser signed them to sit, and they did so in absolute quiet such as only prevailed when they were about to sit for an important examination.

'I shall go over the story of the Norman Conquest,' said Mr Browser, whose brain had been working overtime in order to think of something which might interest the Kiswastis yet keep them guessing as to what it was all about.

'But we've done that already,' came the voice of Anna, much as Mr Browser had expected.

'I know that,' he admitted, 'but I am teaching the Kiswastis as much as you, and when I've reminded you of the story, I shall ask you to act scenes from it—they'll like that.'

So he told the story of how Harold of the

Saxons is supposed to have been tricked by William into promising that he should have the throne, and how William invaded, himself falling on the sand at Pevensey Bay and picking up a handful of it to show that he would win; and how the Saxon farmers all came to Harold's side and the Battle of Hastings was fought on top of a hill.

Ali's uncle perspired as he helped the Kiswasti officials translate what Mr Browser was saying so that the watching Kiswastis could understand a little of what was going on.

Mr Browser drew little pictures on the blackboard to illustrate important points in the story, and the class listened as though none of them had ever heard any of this before, because they wanted to be able to act the scenes well for the Kiswastis.

As for the audience, their telescopes were fixed on the classroom as they listened and watched with genuine fascination. Invasions were completely unknown in their world, where there was only one race, one king and one language.

Following his dramatic story-telling, Mr Browser took a well-earned rest by asking the class to write the story in their own words. This led to some unrest amongst the audience, who after a time found this activity somewhat boring. True, it was interesting to watch Selwyn chewing the end of his pencil and to see a close-up of Anna Cardwell's spidery writing. It was puzzling, too, to wonder what Spiky Jackson had written on the little bit of paper he passed under his desk to Michael. But when Michael put it on his desk, unfolded it and flattened it out, all that Spiky had written was DID YOU BRING YOUR MARBLES WITH YOU? Michael replied by a shake of the head. Soon Mr Browser became aware of the impatience of the Kiswastis, and he stopped wandering around the classroom and called for attention.

'The written work will be continued tomorrow,' he told the class. 'Now let us see how well you have remembered the story by seeing how well you can act it. We'll divide into four groups . . . .'

Mr Browser specified what each group should do, then the groups huddled together and worked out their scenes. The actors and actresses excelled themselves, and the Kiswastis were much affected by Selwyn Jordan's performance as the dying King Harold. The arena was filled again with the Kiswasti hum, showing appreciation as the class filed out of the classroom. As a reward they were allowed to exercise themselves for a while in a playing area, but as this was a bare room, their games were limited to chasing, leapfrog and the like, and they were pleased to be called for their evening meal. Here they were joined by Ali's uncle.

'You have had a great success, Mr Browser,' he said. 'The Kiswastis especially enjoyed the acting of the children.'

'I am glad,' said Mr Browser.

'They like to see something interesting happening all the time. They have heard so much about the wonderful English education, and they are bored with their own lives.'

'Indeed. We will see what we can do,' Mr Browser assured him, thinking that maybe he wasn't the ideal teacher to represent everything modern in English education.

Before the boys settled down for another Kiswasti night, he decided that he would tell them how pleased the Kiswastis were with them. The response was not quite what he had expected.

'If we please them all the time, they'll only keep us here longer,' said Selwyn.

'That's right,' agreed Spiky. 'We ought to bore them to tears—if Kiswastis can cry—Mr Browser. Then they'll become tired of us, and perhaps they'll let us go.'

'Or get rid of us altogether,' put in Michael.

'That's a risk we'll have to take,' said Selwyn seriously. 'I don't want to stay here as a specimen for ever.'

'Nor do we,' echoed the others.

'Bore them?' mused Mr Browser. 'How are we doing to do that?'

'That's easy,' said Spiky. 'Give us only spelling and writing and lots and lots of sums. Read to us from boring books—there are plenty on the shelves. Don't give us anything to do, except perhaps copying down words from the board. They'll surely soon be fed up with us then?'

'I suppose I could do it,' agreed Mr Browser. 'But will you really put up with it? If you start playing about they'll probably find that interesting, too.'

'Don't worry, Mr Browser. We'll be as dead as doornails. Anything to escape from this boring planet!'

'I don't think Mr Sage would approve,' said Mr Browser instinctively.

'Then let him come and teach here,' said Spiky. 'Anyway, some of his lessons are a bit like that. And if they wanted lots of things to happen, why didn't they use Mr Caracco's class? They'd find them more interesting.'

Mr Browser thought this was true. Mr Caracco was young and keen, and the only time his class was still was when he was playing the guitar to them. 'Well, I'll give it a try,' he said doubtfully, 'if you all promise to help.'

'We promise!' they all cried.

'I'll go and see if the girls agree,' said Mr Browser—and they did.

'Something must be done,' declared Miss Copewell. 'I am wasting my time here doing nothing, while down on Earth poor Mr Sage will be getting in such a mess with all those forms and the dinner money!'

'Yes, of course! I hadn't thought of that,' said Mr Browser, and fell asleep rather relieved to think that he wouldn't have to work out any exciting and highly interesting lessons for the next day's session.

7

Spots of Trouble for Spiky

Mr Browser was none too sure the next day whether his most boring lessons were going to be tedious enough for the Kiswastis to demand the return of the class and its replacement with another much more interesting one. The class was playing its part very well. Heads were kept down as notes were copied from text books into exercise books, and when Mr Browser gave long, boring talks about the people who lived in the Middle Ages, everyone listened as though their very lives depended on paying attention—which perhaps they did.

The Kiswasti guards, it is true, were looking worried. Word was getting around that a visit to the museum might not be as entertaining as had been hoped. Ali's uncle walked about with a frown on his forehead most of the time; the numbers attending the sessions were lessening each day. Success, perhaps—but Mr Browser feared lest the irritation of the Kiswastis might lead them into some less pleasant action than sending the humans home.

Then two unexpected events occurred. Spiky Jackson appeared one morning with spots all over his face, and Miss Copewell was called to decide

what kind of spots they were.

'Chicken pox,' she announced. 'Not a serious attack, fortunately, but Simon will have to be isolated for a while.'

Spiky, who apart from the spots was in excellent health, was happy enough to be excused from Mr Browser's boring lessons. The Kiswastis, when they saw Spiky's face, reacted in a highly excitable way. Chicken pox was an illness unknown to them, and Ali's uncle was quickly called so that they could immediately be informed about it.

'Illness,' explained Ali's uncle to Mr Browser and Miss Copewell later, 'is something almost unknown amongst the Kiswastis. There's no knowing what course chicken pox might take if one of them caught the virus. Simon must be kept on his own and approached only by humans.'

So a little private cubicle well away from the others was provided for Spiky, who complained loudly that he felt much too well to be cut off from the rest.

'I'm sorry,' said Mr Browser, 'but it has to be. We can't take any risks, particularly as the illness may be serious for any Kiswasti who catches it.'

'Bother the Kiswastis!' declared Spiky—but he had to obey, and tried to decide whether to read *The Children of the New Forest* or a shortened version of *Ivanhoe*, which appeared to be the most exciting books which Mr Browser had available. A further disadvantage, Spiky discovered, was that his room was next to Ali's uncle, who spent a great deal of him time chanting what Spiky took to be some kind of Eastern prayers, the sound of which became monotonous after the first ten minutes. The only advantage Spiky found in his state was that he was no longer just an exhibit in a museum, though he feared that if his spots didn't die down quickly the Kiswastis might have the idea of exhibiting him on his own.

That afternoon, before the class assembled for their session in the museum, the Kiswasti guards—called guards originally by Anna Cardwell—approached Mr Browser in excited mood.

'The King of the Kiswastis comes today to watch your class,' one of them said. 'He is to decide whether his son, the Prince, is to join your class. He is most keen that his son should learn English. Please see that the class performs well for the King.'

As they lined up to go into the museum area, Mr Browser spoke to the class, some of whom were excited at the thought of being watched by a king.

'We make no change in our plans,' said Mr Browser. 'If we were to please the King too much, he would want to keep us here so that his son could learn English, which might take years.'

'But if we don't please him,' suggested Selwyn, 'he might become angry and punish us—'

'It's a risk we have to take,' replied Mr Browser, and the class walked gloomily into the museum, most of them seeing too clearly that there was no way out of their dilemma.

'They'll keep us here as long as it pleases them,' forecast Anna, 'and then they'll get rid of us—just like they boil down the waxwork figures in Madame Tussaud's when the people aren't famous any more!'

'Quiet, Anna!' ordered Mr Browser angrily, but Anna's grim suggestion had not gone unheard.

The lesson went ahead in the usual boring manner, and the class, in its present mood, found it easy to co-operate. They listened and wrote with earnest faces, their thoughts on the unkindness of fate. At first they tried to see where the Kiswasti King was, but amongst such a huge and distant gathering it was impossible to single him out.

At the end of the lesson one of the Kiswasti guards came to Mr Browser and congratulated him.

'The King was much pleased,' he said. 'The lesson was not of great interest, but because he wants his son to learn with the class, the King requires most to know that hard work is going on.'

That news had a depressing effect upon the class.

'Now we know we shall never go home,' sniffed Anna. 'Whatever we do, they will keep us as objects, even if we stay as still as fossils!'

Michael turned suddenly on little Ali, who was not far from tears, like a number of the others.

'Your uncle caused us to come here!' said Michael, loud enough for everyone to hear. 'It was all his thinking which brought it about. Can't he make up for it, and think us back to Earth?'

'That's right!' Anna agreed. 'Tell him to do something, Ali!'

'It was not his fault!' protested Ali. 'He did not want this to happen. If they had not captured him, they would have found someone else.'

'And that would have been better for us!' declared Martin.

'It's not fair!' complained Ali, and at this point Mr Browser intervened.

'Leave Ali alone,' he demanded. 'We must not start blaming other people, or squabbling amongst ourselves.'

'At least his uncle should try to help us,' persisted Selwyn.

'I would like to see him,' said Ali. 'I am sure he will try.'

'I will ask the guards to let you see him,' said Mr Browser, smiling, 'but I am sure he will not be able to do anything. Somehow we shall have to try to save ourselves. However, I will speak to the Kiswastis tomorrow.'

In the morning, as Mr Browser and Miss Copewell sat with the children eating precisely the same boring breakfast as they had done on each day previously, and Mr Browser was working out the best way to persuade the Kiswastis to let Ali meet his uncle, the meal was interrupted by the arrival of four of the five Kiswasti guards. One of them beckoned with his furry finger to Mr Browser, who rose to join them. The Kiswastis had lost their usual calm, bored appearance, and were chattering to one another as Mr Browser approached them. All the children sensed something unusual, and stopped eating and drinking to take in the encounter.

'Stop there!' called the leading guard when Mr Browser was still five metres away from him. 'Do not come closer. All children must be kept under close control. No one of you must come nearer than this to any Kiswastis!'

His voice was loud enough for all to hear.

'Why not?' asked Mr Browser.

'One Kiswasti ill—perhaps dying!' came the reply.

'I am sorry,' said Mr Browser, 'but—'

'Same illness as the boy,' went on the Kiswasti, and indicated his arms and face. 'Illness not known to Kiswastis—very bad. King will not now send his son to your class. Humans have brought disease to our planet.'

'Is he covered with spots?' asked Mr Browser, dabbing at various parts of his face with his finger, and the Kiswasti nodded.

'It must be chicken pox,' Mr Browser declared, 'and that is a harmless illness.'

'Not to Kiswastis,' said the guard. 'Kiswastis have no diseases, so any disease very bad. Kiswasti may die from it.'

'We will keep our children together and under our control,' Mr Browser promised. 'I hope your friend will recover. Now I have a request to make.'

'Request?'

'Yes, something to ask you. The boy whose uncle caused us to come here would like to speak to him.'

The Kiswastis shook their heads, then chattered again together. At length the English-speaking one stepped forward.

'The uncle will come to speak with boy, but boy must stay away from him, so that no disease can be passed.'

'Oh, thank you!' called out Ali, and Mr Browser came back to join the children. The Kiswastis beat a hasty retreat.

'Now what will they do to us?' asked Anna tearfully as they gathered to go for the next lesson. 'If they think we have brought them a disease, maybe they'll want to be rid of us.'

'It's only one person affected so far,' said Mr Browser, 'and Spiky has been isolated, so it should make no difference.'

There was the usual audience that morning, so

evidently the news of the illness of the Kiswasti guard had not been spread around. The Kiswastis had to find what interest they could in the differing styles of the children's writing, or in their expressions while they listened to Mr Browser; even he was disturbed by the lifelessness of his class, which he knew was not so much caused by boredom now as by a growing sense of hopelessness. Few of them now believed they had any chance of returning home.

At the end of the lesson, back in their quarters, Ali's uncle, Fazal Khan, appeared outside their room, and the guards beckoned Ali to approach him, but would not allow him less than three paces away.

'Now, Ali—you wish to speak to me?' began his uncle.

'Yes, Uncle, we are tired of being here, and want to return to Earth. My friends are saying that by your thinking you have brought us here, so in the same way you should arrange for our return.'

Fazal Khan's white beard wobbled as he broke into a high pitched laugh.

'It was one thing to cause you to be brought here, my boy, but quite another to persuade the Kiswastis to let you go.'

'But you must try, Uncle, please!'

'Oh, I will try, my boy, but it is not easy.' Suddenly he broke into Urdu. 'Tell Mr Browser he should come and see the boy Spiky Jackson in one hour's time. And if the Kiswastis want to know what I have said, tell them I was saying a prayer for you in our own language.'

'I will. Goodbye, Uncle,' said Ali, speaking in English again.

The guards did not question Ali, but they stepped forward and urged him back to the others.

'Not much hope, I suppose,' said Michael. 'He's a prisoner as much as we are.'

When the guards had gone, Ali went up to Mr Browser.

'My uncle asks that you visit Simon in one hour's time,' he said.

'I've already visited him today, and so has Miss Copewell,' said Mr Browser.

'But my uncle wishes it—he told me so secretly,' insisted Ali. 'Perhaps he has some plan.'

'The guards will stop me,' objected Mr Browser.

'Perhaps my uncle knows that they are busy at that time. He must badly want to talk with you.'

'All right, Ali, I'll try. I'll have to pretend I'm sleepwalking,' said Mr Browser, smiling, though he was really far from amused.

At the appointed time he crept along the corridor, turned to the right down another one, and then to the left, and stood outside Spiky's cubicle.

'How are you, Simon?' he whispered.

Spiky came at once to the transparent panel in the door, through which sound passed as easily as vision.

'I'm all right, Mr Browser, but it's boring in here. When can I come out again?'

Mr Browser told him about the illness of the Kiswasti guard.

'You'll have to be prepared to stay on here for some time yet,' he told Spiky. 'They won't take any risks with us now. The King was going to let his son join the class, but I'm sure he won't do that now.'

'I saw the Prince come by here with the guards,' said Spiky. 'He looked a jolly little fellow, with furry fingers and a furry nose. I'm sure he'd understand about us wanting to go home. Somebody should see the King—'

'Ssshhhh!' A quiet hissing sound caused Mr Browser to turn round. Fazal Khan was standing there, blowing through his yellow teeth.

'I have a message for you,' he said, and pushed a piece of paper into Mr Browser's hand. 'Now you must go straight back, for the guards will soon be returning to bring this boy his food. He is well looked after—but do not be surprised if something happens to him!'

'Something happens? What do you mean?'

'Go at once, there is no time to lose—and hide the paper away, the guards must not see it. Go!'

109

And Fazal tried to help Mr Browser on his way.

'Tell them they'd better let me go, Mr Browser!' called out Spiky, and Fazal hissed through his teeth again and urged Mr Browser away. Then he turned back to Spiky.

'Be patient, boy,' he said. 'You have to learn that time can be on your side. Eat your meal when the guard brings it, and I will be back again—quicker than you think!'

He moved silently away, leaving Spiky alone and not much cheered up by either Fazal's or Mr Browser's words. As for Mr Browser, he returned at once to his sleeping quarters and took out the note Fazal had given him. This he read several times, now and then raising his eyebrows and frowning. Then he walked round the room with his hands behind his back and his head held high— a stance he sometimes took up when considering what to do with boys who had badly misbehaved themselves. With a final shake of the head, he went out to inspect the children in their rooms. The light soon faded, and some of the class fell into uneasy sleep, while others stared into the darkness and were sorry for themselves.

For the first time since their arrival on the planet of the Kiswastis, the short night was abruptly disturbed. They woke to the sound of running feet and Kiswasti chattering. Their rooms were suddenly flooded with artificial light. Mr Browser came running from his room to see what was going on in the boys' bedroom, and Miss Copewell sat up anxiously, ready to try and protect the girls.

'What's wrong?' Mr Browser called to the guards—but they ignored him and began a thorough search of the rooms. Only when they had finished, their efforts clearly in vain, did the English-speaking guard address Mr Browser.

'The boy with the spots is missing,' he said. 'He is not in his room. This is most dangerous and very wrong. All Kiswastis could become seriously ill if the disease spreads. Have any of you seen him?'

Heads were shaken and some denied having seen Spiky.

'My mum says chicken pox is not infectious after the spots have come out,' called out Anna, but this did not comfort the guards, who stood there at a loss what to do next.

Another pair of feet came shuffling hastily down the corridor. Fazal Khan arrived, panting and excited.

'The boy has left me a message,' he said. 'He says he has gone to beg the King's son to persuade his father to let the children return to Earth.'

'The King's son!' The English-speaking Kiswasti reverted to his own language, and the others chattered so fast that they were in danger of choking; it was their way of showing fear. Suddenly they all turned and ran away, leaving the

111

children, Mr Browser, Miss Copewell and Ali's uncle standing where they had gathered together, staring after the Kiswastis.

'Poor Spiky,' said Thelma. 'Whatever will they do to him if they catch him?'

'It is a crisis,' said Fazal Khan. 'I must go back and do some more thinking.'

Ali thought he saw his uncle wink at Mr Browser, but he said nothing, because he could hardly believe it. His uncle was not usually a winking man.

8

An Art Lesson in Space

'This morning,' said Mr Browser, after the class had settled down in the classroom of the Museum of Other Worlds, 'we will have an art lesson. I would like you all to experiment with shades of the colour red. I want you to mix all kinds of colours with it, even perhaps thickening the paint with chalk or paste. Try any experiment you like, and then create some kind of pattern with your colour. Remember, great painters like Van Gogh used very thick paint in order to obtain their effects. Don't be afraid to try things out—I shall be looking for a wide variety of shades of red when I come round to look at your work. Paste and chalks are available at the front—now set those Kiswastis guessing.'

The works of Vincent Van Gogh were as unknown to Class 8 as to the watching Kiswastis, but both the class and the watchers became deeply involved in the work as the experiment began. Mr Browser moved quietly around as the paints were mixed, pointing and having a quiet word here and there. What the Kiswastis did not realise was that Mr Browser was whispering much the same thing to each group of painters.

'I'm looking for a certain colour,' he said, 'and it

has to be made with a thick mixture. It could be vital for our lives to find exactly the right shade. That's much too runny, Anna. Add a little white chalk—'

The class worked with complete concentration, and the Kiswasti audience was greatly impressed. Red was not a prevalent colour on their planet, and the shades the children were producing were largely unknown to them. The lesson was not without its mishaps, of course, as any art lesson in an ordinary classroom cannot be. Michael spilt his paint on the floor and it had to be mopped up by his group, and Selwyn smeared paint from his fingers all over one side of his face.

'Please, Mr Browser, where can I wash it off?' he asked, when the laughter of the rest of his group revealed to him what had happened. To his surprise, Mr Browser didn't tell him off, nor for a while did he advise him what to do; he stood and stared at the paint on Selwyn's face.

'That's it!' he whispered.'Just what I want! How much of this mixture have you made, Selwyn?'

'There's plenty of it in that jam jar, Mr Browser.'

'Good. Go and clean up your face at the tap over in the corner, and on the way back bring the pot with the lid on it from my desk. Let it lie on your desk for a while, and when attention is not so much on you, fill the pot with the same mixture and fit the lid on tightly. I shall come around

115

shortly afterwards and remove it. Got that?'

'Yes, Mr Browser.' Puzzled, Selwyn did as he was told. Five minutes later Mr Browser quietly pocketed the pot with Selwyn's mixture in it, then went on criticising the efforts of the class.

The watching Kiswastis were enthusiastic about the shades and patterns produced by the class. This was one of Mr Browser's more lively lessons, even having been praised by an Art Organiser, and the display of patterns Mr Browser put around the room brought a buzz of Kiswasti conversation. But as the class was filing out of the museum, suddenly a loud announcement silenced the crowd. Silence fell in the huge arena, and then the

Kiswastis began very earnestly and quietly to leave.

'I wonder what they've been told,' mused Anna. 'Something serious must have happened.'

'I wonder if the Kiswasti guard has died,' said Selwyn. 'If he has, the Kiswastis won't like the idea of Spiky being at large. I wonder where he is!'

When they returned to their living quarters, Ali's uncle was waiting for Mr Browser.

'The guard has died,' he announced, 'and all the Kiswastis have been warned that the boy Simon is trying to contact the Prince. A state of emergency has been declared, the Kiswastis are so afraid lest the disease spreads.'

'Poor Simon,' said Mr Browser. 'We must hope that he falls into the hands of sensible Kiswastis who will send him back here.'

'Yes, yes, it is to be hoped,' agreed Fazal Khan. 'Now I must leave you to return to the search for him. I must try to see the King, to persuade him that the poor boy will bring no harm to anyone if he is sent straight back here.'

'I do hope you are successful!' said Miss Copewell, who had never found life more confusing. 'I feel so sorry for the poor boy, alone on a strange planet with no one to help him.'

'Aren't we all like that?' observed Anna, and Miss Copewell frowned and decided to ignore her.

The quick Kiswasti twilight fell, and still there

117

was no news of Spiky. The guards were on edge, and determined that no more children should escape. They were all sent to bed and told to lie quietly, and not before then did the guards feel that they could be safely left alone.

Some of the class lay sobbing quietly, partly for Spiky but mostly for themselves, for like Anna they realised that in effect their position was as hopeless as his. Half an hour later many of them were still awake when a slight rustling disturbed the peace of the room, as Mr Browser and Miss Copewell moved quietly into the girls' room.

'Wake up!' whispered Miss Copewell, an order which was unnecessary for most of the girls, who were still wide awake. 'Listen to Mr Browser, please!'

'Girls,' said Mr Browser, 'we are going to come and choose several of you to help us scare the Kiswastis into sending us home. I have here some paint, and I'm going to dab it on the faces of six girls so that they will look as if they are coming out in chicken pox spots. Six out of sixteen will be enough. The Kiswastis will then be afraid that more of you will develop spots later on. Don't fuss—be ever so quiet. Miss Copewell has a small torch which she will shine on your faces while I do the make-up work.'

Mr Browser then produced a small brush and Selwyn'x mixture of paint, and set to work on

118

Anna Cardwell's face, planting spots on both cheeks and her forehead.

'How's that?' he asked Miss Copewell after working carefully for a full five minutes.

'It looks a bad case to me,' declared Miss Copewell, and Anna giggled.

'Lie still, and whatever you do, don't smear the paint,' Mr Browser warned her. 'It's a thick mixture, but it could be a matter of life or death. The Kiswastis must believe that chicken pox has broken out.'

'I promise not to move all night, Mr Browser,'

declared Anna, and she did her best to keep her promise, even after she fell asleep.

Six girls and eight boys received the treatment, and it was the middle of the Kiswasti night before Mr Browser and Miss Copewell went to bed—not to sleep, but to pray that the chicken pox victims would not upset their spots! By arrangement with Mr Browser, Miss Copewell rose every hour or so and went with him on an inspection of the spotted faced children, checking to make sure that the paint had not run or been smeared while the victims slept. Miss Copewell applied a damp cloth to one or two of the spots, but in the main there was no need for touching up work, for those who dozed for a while had slept on their backs, making sure the spots were not disturbed.

To Mr Browser and to Miss Copewell, as well as to many of the children, that night seemed the longest of their lives, although it was only a short Kiswasti one. At last, though, the sudden dawn arrived. Each member of the class, spotted or not, lay tensely awake, sensing that something must be about to happen. Mr Browser and Miss Copewell could be heard talking in the corridor between the rooms. Each then made a hasty inspection, and warned the children to remain where they were.

Promptly, as usual, the Kiswasti guards appeared.

'Please!' the children heard Mr Browser call.

'You must look at these children. They have caught the illness which the missing boy has!'

The English-speaking guard warned Mr Browser to keep his distance, then he and his comrades put their heads nervously round the doors to the children's rooms.

'Those children who have spots, sit up,' said Mr Browser. The guards took one look, and all heads were withdrawn. There followed a gabble of Kiswasti conversation.

'All children to remain where they are!' ordered the English-speaking guard, and left hastily with the rest of them.

'What's happening, Mr Browser?' called out Michael.

'I'm not sure,' said Mr Browser. 'We must wait and see. Well done, but you must try to keep those spots in perfect condition for a little longer.'

'They won't dare come near us,' declared Selwyn. 'They're scared stiff of us!'

'But what will they do?' asked Michael anxiously. Mr Browser shrugged his shoulders.

'Be patient,' was all he would say. A quarter of an hour passed, then sounds of running feet were heard. Ali's Uncle Fazal appeared, puffing and panting, and followed at a safe distance by the guards.

'The King has given a command,' he announced, 'that we are to be returned to Earth

immediately, before the chicken pox can spread to the Kiswastis. They are already preparing the space craft, and you must all go straight to it. There is no time for washing or eating. Straight to the craft!'

The English-speaking guard was nodding agreement, clearly eager to be rid of these threats to the Kiswasti health. Some of the children started to cheer, but Mr Browser quickly squashed that.

'Dress quickly and line up,' he ordered them. 'We don't want to risk a change of mind.'

'Just as well we don't have to wash,' whispered Selwyn, looking at Michael's spots. In two minutes they were all lined up in the corridor.

'Ready,' said Mr Browser, and the guards waved them to start walking, themselves keeping well ahead of them out of reach of the dreaded germs.

Suddenly Anna, who was in the middle of the line, blocked the progress of those behind her by stopping short.

'We can't go!' she called out, and Miss Copewell rushed at once to hurry her up.

'You must!' she whispered. 'We dare not delay! You want to go back home, don't you?'

'Yes, but where's Spiky? We can't just leave Spiky behind!'

'That's right,' agreed Michael. 'Spiky must come too!'

And others slowed up and voiced their agreement. Mr Browser and Ali's uncle hurried back to reason with the waverers.

'It's your only chance,' said Mr Browser. 'We don't know where Simon is—it's because they don't want any more of you to escape like him that they're sending you home. I'm afraid it's many lives against one.'

'Indeed,' added Fazal Khan, 'your friend Spiky may be able to follow us later—'

'Move!' demanded the guard, and all further discussion was stopped.

The children marched silently back the way they had first come, glad to be going yet sadly missing Spiky. They entered the space craft, to which the grab had already been attached, and were prepared for the return journey through space. To the last moment some hoped that Spiky would appear, and when the craft took off, there were tears from many of the homegoing humans. Ali's uncle was with them this time, and once the craft was under way, he winked at Ali.

Ali thought, for the first time, that his uncle was a horrid man.

9

Reunion in Space

After being primed with pills for various purposes, and following a night when few had enjoyed much sleep, most of the party soon slipped into unconsciousness on the journey homeward from the planet of the Kiswastis.

Mr Browser, struggling with his conscience over the desertion of Simon Jackson, withstood the power of the drugs for a while. To return to Earth with all but one of his class was an unexpected pleasure, yet he couldn't help worrying about the one missing sheep. How could he explain the absence of Spiky to the boy's parents, if the party did reach home in safety? He couldn't expect them to be pleased with the explanation that it was better to save twenty nine children and lose the thirtieth, than to lose them all. In fact, it would be extremely difficult, decided Mr Browser dozily, to explain any of the events that had happened since the *Kiswasti* sank. Fazal Khan was stretched out alongside him, and he made a last attempt to contact him, but Fazal, when his arm was shaken, only briefly opened his eyes, winked at Mr Browser and closed them again. The fellow was no use at all, decided Mr Browser, and slipped into unconsciousness himself.

As on the outward journey, the tired children lying on a soft surface and in a pleasantly conditioned atmosphere, were able to sleep for most of the journey through outer space. Unknown to them, as the craft approached to a few million miles from the oxygen belt of the Earth, their speed diminished and the Kiswasti crew set about certain tasks to ensure a correct and speedy landing for their human cargo.

The atmosphere in the area accommodating the children gradually changed, so that they were invigorated rather than kept in a drowsy condition. As the adults awoke, the ladder which had descended from the grab on the outward flight came down again. Fazal Khan suddenly became very excited, jumped to his feet and ran around waking the children.

'We must climb up the ladder!' he kept on saying. 'That is the way out. They will put us down from there—here, we cannot get out!'

The whole class was enthusiastic—there was no difficulty in persuading them.

'Let's go!' cried Michael, and made a rush for the ladder.

'No, no!' ordered Mr Browser. 'One at a time, or someone will be hurt falling into the grab!'

They remembered how they had tumbled out

of it, and allowed themselves to be organised. Miss Copewell and Fazal Khan were the first to go, to try and ease the fall for those who followed.

'Oh, my!' they heard Miss Copewell call out as she slid into the grab. 'What a surprise!'

Fazal Khan laughed and waved to them as he followed her, and then the children began to disappear from the top of the ladder. There was a great commotion from inside the grab, and suddenly all progress was halted. Selwyn stood uncertainly at the top.

'Hurry up!' urged Anna. 'We don't want to be left behind.'

Then a face appeared over the claw-like edge of the grab.

'Spiky!' cried Anna.

'Yes, it's me,' called out Spiky. 'Ali's uncle is holding me up. Nice to see you, Mr Browser!'

'Spiky! Where have you been?' demanded Mr Browser, amazed enough to forget to call him Simon.

'I've been in here all the time,' said Spiky. 'Ali's uncle took me here and hid me.'

'But how—' began Selwyn.

'I'll explain everything later,' declared Spiky. 'I'm a bit of a weight for him to hold up— you'd better hurry up and come in here, if you want to be set free!'

And the smiling face, encased in a transparent helmet, disappeared. The transfer from the space travelling room to the grab was now quickly completed, and the grab closed again.

'You can take that off now,' said Fazal Khan to Spiky. 'Oxygen is now being supplied in the grab to all of us.'

Spiky removed his helmet, and his companions gave him three cheers—to his surprise.

'How did you get here, Spiky?' demanded Michael, and the others, awkwardly hunched together as they were, all listened expectantly.

'He deserved your cheers,' said Fazal Khan,

'because without him we should not be here now.'

'But for Ali's uncle we shouldn't be,' called out Spiky. 'He organised everything—let him tell you all about it. He knows more than I do.'

'Yes, tell us, Uncle Fazal!' demanded Ali, pleased to find that his uncle had suddenly become more popular.

'Well, it is like this,' began Fazal. 'When Spiky—Simon that is—fell ill, and the Kiswasti guard caught the disease from him, and was growing worse every hour, I saw how excited and upset the rest of the Kiswastis were. When the guard died, and the King changed his mind about having his son in your class, I thought that perhaps Spiky's illness could be used to help us all. I went straight to the King, and told him that more children were likely to catch chicken pox, and that if the disease were allowed to spread it might in the end reach his own son. He said that he would like to send us all home, but that he would not yet be able to persuade the others. I then proposed, through his interpreter, that Spiky should disappear, which would strike fear into the other Kiswastis. I also told Mr Browser to make chicken pox spots appear on the faces of other children. This he did most excellently!'

'Yes—but where did Spiky go?' asked Anna.

'Ha ha! Yes, where did Spiky go?' Fazal Khan was enjoying himself thoroughly. 'With the help of the King I secretly took Spiky at night to this very spot. I persuaded the King to arrange for Spiky to be hidden in this grab. One of the Kiswasti technicians was ordered to open it up, and Spiky crept inside. He has been here ever since, breathing through his special space helmet. A very brave boy, I must say. Then, when all the other chicken pox spots were discovered, the Kiswastis, in a panic, went to the King to demand that the whole party of humans should be removed, before the disease spread. The King suggested that the party could be sent back to Earth, and arrangements were made for the flight at once. So here we are, and you may now rub off the spots so cleverly applied by Mr Browser and Miss Copewell!'

'Three cheers for Mr Khan!' cried Spiky, and led the cheering, in which Mr Browser and Miss Copewell joined.

'Thank you very much,' said Fazal Khan politely. 'Now, I think, we must be ready to land. It will not be very comfortable, I think, being dropped as if out of a lion's mouth to the ground!'

Nobody was very much worried about whether the landing would be a soft one or not, as long as they could know that they were on

Mother Earth again. The grab shuddered, and they felt as if they were in a huge lift as it swung upwards and outwards. Then, suddenly, it dipped, its jaws opened, and out they tumbled. The landing was soft and wet, not at all as they had expected. When they recovered themselves and stood on their feet, the craft was already shooting upwards, the grab already withdrawn on top of the craft.

'Home again!' cried Anna—but when Mr Browser looked around him, he knew that their difficulties were not yet over. They had been put back on the same sandbank on which the *Kiswasti* had sunk.

'We're back on the sandbank!' Anna confirmed. 'They should have dropped us back at school!'

But the others were too busy dancing joyfully on the wet sand to take any notice of her. Selwyn was the first to calm down and face the truth.

'The water's spreading across the sand,' he pointed out to Mr Browser. 'Only slowly, but we don't know whether this sandbank is always here, or how deeply the water can cover it.'

Spiky and Michael watched the water as it proved that Selwyn was right. Their island was gradually becoming smaller.

'We'll have to attract somebody else's attention,' said Michael. 'Surely a fishing boat or a yacht will come this way soon.'

But the mouth of the little River Graywater was not a popular place for boating, and it was a depressing sight to the castaways. Not a boat was on the water, and the banks of the river were the edges of long stretches of marshland, where birds were the only creatures visible.

'What time is it?' asked Anna. Consulting their watches was no use, for they had not kept pace with the Kiswasti time, and had been upset by the different magnetic forces on that planet.

'It's hard to tell the time because of the clouds,' said Mr Browser, 'but the light is certainly growing stronger. I would say, considering the time of year, it's about half past five in the morning.'

'No wonder nobody's about,' said Anna.

'How many days have we been away?' asked Martin.

'Hard to say,' admitted Mr Browser. 'My sense of time seems all upset.'

'Maybe the Kiswastis can play about with time,' suggested Selwyn, 'then it could be only the morning after we were taken away.'

'I'm starving,' observed the more practical Michael, and others agreed. Discussions about time didn't seem very important to them, and some began to yell for help.

'Waste of time,' said Spiky. 'The breeze is blowing offshore.'

'We'll have to hope that someone will pass this way sooner or later,' said Mr Browser not too hopefully.

'Who would want to come here?' said Anna, and the others gloomily had to agree that a submerging sandbank at the mouth of the River Graywater was not the kind of place to attract visitors.

'There's a farmhouse away on the left bank,' said Michael, pointing to the place which the captain of the *Kiswasti* had called at after his ship broke up.

'Yes—and there's smoke coming out of the chimney,' added Spiky. 'Somebody's living there, for sure.'

'That's a lot of good to us!' grumbled Michael. 'They'll never realise that we're stuck out here, drown—'

'Quiet, Michael!' ordered Mr Browser.

'Fancy going all that way into space, and then coming back and drowning on a silly sandbank!' said Anna, sniffing.

'Quiet, Anna!' said Mr Browser half-heartedly; clearly Anna had only spoken what the others suspected in their hearts.

Spiky Jackson took off his shoes and socks,

and followed this by stripping to his shorts. He was so quick that this was all done before Miss Copewell or Mr Browser saw what was happening. He stepped into the water and waded out until the water was waist high.

'Simon!' cried Mr Browser. 'What are you doing? Come back at once!'

Spiky shook his head.

'I've been practising long distance swimming,' he said. 'I reckon I can easily reach the shore from here. I'll run to the farm and tell them we're here. It could be our only chance.'

'Simon! I forbid you!'

Spiky's answer was to turn away from Mr Browser, plunge into the water and start swimming. Mr Browser ran into the water as if hoping to reach him and pull him back, but he wasn't a strong swimmer, and Spiky was soon too far away to make it worth while trying to catch him. Mr Browser returned with his trousers dripping.

'That boy is always causing trouble,' he complained, a little unjustly. 'I do hope that he makes it to the shore!'

The whole group lined the sandbank and watched as Spiky's arms appeared and disappeared as he swam away from them. Soon he was only a dot in the sea—a dot which disappeared for longer and longer periods.

'Spiky's a strong swimmer, Mr Browser,' said Michael. Mr Browser nodded, and after that no one spoke for a very long time. They stood in the same place, looking, and did not notice as the water surrounded their feet and began to lap round their ankles.

Spiky swam confidently, trying not to waste his energy, and aware that he was making good progress. The water was reasonably calm, for which he was thankful, and all went well until he became aware of a strong current which began to drag him away from the left bank of the estuary and towards the deserted shore on his right hand.

He gritted his teeth and fought against it, but the effort was energy sapping, just what he wanted to avoid. For a time he hardly made any progress at all, and he began to wish he had never left the sandbank. Suppose he drowned, and then the rest were saved? Too late to consider such thoughts! He just had to keep on going. He changed to the breast stroke, and made slow but steady progress, but now and again his legs began to drag as his arm movements became weaker.

Exhaustion made him ready to give up trying to make progress, and he changed to a tired dog paddle. His legs sank down lower in the water—and his foot dragged against something solid. He swam forward a couple of strokes and then lowered his feet again; they touched a sandy surface. Joyfully he tried to stand up. The water came up to his neck—but he had reached land. He still had a quarter of a mile to go, but thanks to the estuary sandbanks he was able to reach the shore, now swimming, now walking, quite easily.

He flung himself on the muddy beach and breathed in deeply for a few seconds, then sprang to his feet and set off towards the farmhouse. Ten minutes later he was at the farmyard gate, and the farmer's dog proclaimed that he did not approve of the appearance of the skinny swimmer. The dog's barking alerted the farmer, who opened the door and stared in surprise at Spiky.

'Where have you come from?' he demanded.

'Out there,' explained Spiky, pointing. 'From the sandbank. All my friends are out there, and Mr Browser and Miss Copewell—and Fazal Khan!'

'The missing children!' said the farmer. 'How on earth have you survived there all night?'

'Not on Earth—' began Spiky, but decided he'd better not waste time trying to explain. 'The water's closing in on the sandbank,' he said. 'Can somebody go out there quickly?'

'Of course!' The farmer dialled 999 and gave

an urgent message to the police. By this time his wife had wrapped Spiky in a blanket and provided him with some hot tea.

'Is it only one night since the boat sank?' asked Spiky.

'Yes, my dear, and I think you're lucky to be alive—thanks to those shifting sandbanks. No one knows what they're going to do next!'

First a speedboat was sent out to the sandbank, to make sure that the stranded party was still safe, and this was followed by a large motorboat, big enough to rescue the whole group. News of the rescue was flashed to Chivvy Chase School, and from there to all the parents, now as overwhelmed with joy as they had been with grief.

Spiky was later presented with an award for bravery by the Parents' Association—a football signed by all the members of his local football team. It was also hinted that people have been presented at Buckingham Palace for less—but nothing has been said to Spiky about it yet.

Some of the children said nothing about the Kiswastis, fearing that they wouldn't be believed. Those who did received doubting looks, or were told that spending a night on a wet sandbank must have caused them to have strange dreams.

In class, Mr Browser was questioned about

the short time which had passed between the sinking of the *Kiswasti* and their return to the sandbank.

'It's very hard to explain,' said Mr Browser.

'Do you think the Kiswastis can control our time?' asked Anna brightly.

'Either that, or they can control our idea of time.'

'I hope their fear of chicken pox and other diseases keeps them away,' said Michael. 'How's your chicken pox, Spiky?'

'All vanished,' said Spiky, and then he looked closely at Michael's face. 'But I think it's your turn now, Mike. Those two spots look genuine, not like Mr Browser's painted ones.'

So Michael had to be sent home—a very down-to-earth ending to an unearthly story. Not quite the end, perhaps. Mr Watchett was still worried about all those missing chairs and desks, and was wondering whether he ought not to retire and make way for a younger man. Then Mr Sage received a phone call early the next morning from a park keeper.

'I've just found a pile of chairs and desks dumped in the children's playground here,' he reported. 'Some of them have "C.C." written underneath them in chalk. Could they belong to Chivvy Chase School?'

'I'll come and have a look,' said Mr Sage,

and he took Mr Watchett to inspect the pile of furniture.

'That's them,' said Mr Watchett, greatly relieved. 'It was vandals all the time, I suppose, Mr Sage!'

'Of course,' agreed Mr Sage, and they arranged to have the chairs and desks returned, damaged though many of them were.

Now Mr Watchett knew very well in his heart that vandals had not been responsible; he could imagine the huge grab descending and dropping the desks and chairs back on Earth. But, like many people before him who have seen strange things, he was afraid, and preferred to explain things away by finding some ordinary cause. So the Kiswastis and the grab were soon forgotten by Mr Watchett, who came in the end to believe himself that it was all the fault of vandals.

One other little matter worried Spiky for a while, until one day he cornered little Ali Khan in the playground.

'Ali—what happened to your Uncle Fazal?' he asked.

'Oh, he's gone back to Pakistan,' said Ali. 'They said he was an illegal immigrant.'

'What's that?'

'They said he'd come into the country without any papers,' said Ali, 'which was, of course,

true.'

'That's not fair,' said Spiky. 'We didn't have any papers either.

'Oh, my uncle was pleased,' said Ali. 'He wanted to go back there. He doesn't like our climate at all. He said it's no good for thinking. I expect he's sitting under a tree out there, thinking, at this very moment.'

'I hope he's leaving us and the Kiswastis out

of his thinking,' declared Spiky. 'That sort of thinking is too dangerous.'

'Sometimes,' said Ali, laughing, 'I like to sit and think, too. It's more exciting than playing football.'

Spiky gave him a suspicious look, concluded that Ali was joking, and decided that at the moment football, not thinking, was for him.

Other Titles in Andersen Young Readers' Library

Pamela Blackie	*Jinny the Witch Flies Over the House*
Roy Brown	*A Nag Called Wednesday*
Frank Charles	*Beyond the Midnight Mountains*
Roger Collinson	*Get Lavinia Goodbody!* *Paper Flags and Penny Ices*
Philip Curtis	*A Party for Lester* *Beware of the Brain Sharpeners* *Mr Browser and the Brain Sharpeners* *Mr Browser and the Comet Crisis* *Mr Browser and the Mini-Meteorites* *The Revenge of the Brain Sharpeners*
Elfie Donnelly	*Odd Stockings* *So Long, Grandpa*
Peter Hartling	*Theo Runs Away*
Geoffrey Hayes	*Patrick Comes to Puttyville*
Hans-Eric Hellberg	*The One-Eyed Bandits*
J. K. Hooper	*Kaspar and the Iron Poodle*

Gudrun Mebs	*Sunday's Child*
Christine Nostlinger	*Conrad*
	Lollipop
	Mr Bat's Great Invention
Jan Procházka	*The Carp*
Nora Rock	*Monkey's Perfect*
John Singleton	*The Adventures of Muckpup*
Brenda Sivers	*Biminy in Danger*
Angela Sommer-Bodenburg	*The Little Vampire*
	The Little Vampire Moves In
	The Little Vampire Takes a Trip
Robert Taylor	*The Dewin*
	The Line of Dunes
David Tinkler	*The Snoots Strike Back*
Hazel Townson	*Haunted Ivy*
	The Choking Peril
	The Great Ice-Cream Crime
	The Shrieking Face
	The Siege of Cobb Street School
	The Speckled Panic
	The Vanishing Gran
Ursula Moray Williams	*Jeffy, the Burglar's Cat*
M. A. Wood	*Master Deor's Apprentice*